LEISURE ARTS PRESENTS

O Christmas tree

LEISURE ARTS, INC.
Little Rock, Arkansas

EDITORIAL STAFF

Editor: Anne Van Wagner Childs. *Executive Director:* Sandra Graham Case. *Creative Art Director:* Gloria Bearden. *Executive Editor:* Susan Frantz Wiles. PRODUCTION — *Managing Editor:* Carla Bentley. *Senior Editor:* Susan Sullivan. *Project Coordinator:* Kelley R. Pillow. EDITORIAL — *Associate Editor:* Dorothy Latimer Johnson. *Senior Editorial Writer:* Laurie R. Burleson. *Editorial Writer:* Barbara Cameron Ford. *Editorial Copy Assistant:* Linda L. Trimble. *Advertising and Direct Mail Copywriters:* Steven M. Cooper and Marla Shivers. ART — *Production Art Director:* Melinda Stout. *Senior Production Artist:* Stephen L. Mooningham. *Chart Production Artists:* Paul Allen, Diane Ghegan, Leslie Loring Krebs, Martha Jordan, Michael Spigner, and Cindy A. Zimmerebner-Johnson. *Photography Stylists:* Sondra Harrison Daniel, Karen Smart Hall, Judith Howington Merritt, Charlisa Erwin Parker, and Christina Tiano. *Typesetters:* Cindy Lumpkin and Stephanie Cordero. *Advertising and Direct Mail Artist:* Linda Lovette.

BUSINESS STAFF

Publisher: Steve Patterson. *Controller:* Tom Siebenmorgen. *Retail Sales Director:* Richard Tignor. *Retail Marketing Director:* Pam Stebbins. *Retail Customer Services Director:* Margaret Sweetin. *Marketing Manager:* Russ Barnett. *Executive Director of Marketing and Circulation:* Guy A. Crossley. *Fulfillment Manager:* Byron L. Taylor. *Print Production:* Nancy Reddick Lister and Laura Lockhart.

CREDITS

PHOTOGRAPHY: Ken West, Larry Pennington, Mark Mathews, and Karen Busick Shirey of Peerless Photography, Little Rock, Arkansas; and Jerry Davis Photography, Little Rock, Arkansas. COLOR SEPARATIONS: Magna IV Engravers of Little Rock, Arkansas. CUSTOM FRAMING: Nelda and Carlton Newby of Creative Framers, North Little Rock, Arkansas. PHOTO ACCESSORIES: Crocus Flowers and Gifts of Little Rock, Arkansas, fireplace mantel, page 45.

International Standard Book Number 0-942237-15-3

INTRODUCTION

Our most beloved holiday decoration, the Christmas tree has held a special place in our hearts and homes for more than a century. Though German immigrants brought it to our country as early as the 1700's, most Americans did not adopt the custom until it became popular in Victorian England. When Prince Albert, Queen Victoria's German husband, decorated an evergreen tree at Christmastime, the Victorians responded by reproducing the splendor of the royal tree in their own homes. It wasn't long before it became fashionable in America as well. With the help of the ladies' publications of the day, families spent many happy hours creating imaginative decorations. Famous authors of the time, such as Charles Dickens and Hans Christian Andersen, immortalized the Victorian Christmas tree forever by describing its bountiful branches.

In O Christmas Tree, we honor the Victorians' contributions to the decorated evergreen. Many of the designs in this book were inspired by postcards, lithographs, and ornamental scraps from that era. It is our hope that this cross stitch collection will bring old-fashioned charm to your Yuletide celebration, now and for many years to come.

TABLE OF CONTENTS

O Christmas Tree

I have been looking on, this evening, at a merry company of children assembled round that pretty German toy, a Christmas tree. The tree was planted in the middle of a great round table, and towered high above their heads. It was brilliantly lighted by a multitude of little tapers; and everywhere sparkled and glittered with bright objects. There were rosy-cheeked dolls, hiding behind green leaves; there were real watches (with movable hands, at least, and an endless capacity of being wound up) dangling from innumerable twigs; there were French-polished tables, chairs, bedsteads, wardrobes, eight-day clocks and various other articles of domestic furniture (wonderfully made in tin) perched among the boughs, as if in preparation for some fairy housekeeping; there were jolly broad-faced little men, much more agreeable in appearance than many real men — and no wonder, for their heads come off and showed them to be full of sugarplums; there were trinkets for the elder girls, far brighter than any grown-up gold and jewels; there were baskets and pincushions in all devices; there were guns, swords, and banners; there were witches standing in enchanted rings of pasteboard, to tell fortunes; there were teetotums, humming-tops, needle cases, pen wipers, smelling-bottles, conversation-cards, bouquet holders, real fruit made artificially dazzling with gold leaf; imitation apples, pears, walnuts crammed with surprises; in short, as a pretty child, before me, delightedly whispered to another pretty child, her bosom friend, "There was everything, and more."

— CHARLES DICKENS

Chart on pages 48-49

Childhood Legacy

The excitement of children at Christmas is a joy to behold as they discover the toys Santa has delivered just for them. Because alphabet blocks are an imaginative way to learn and play — an idea embraced by the Victorians — they were especially popular gifts during that era. The charming collection here is a nostalgic tribute to the playfulness and creativity of children everywhere — and to the dear old Santa who loves them so.

Charts on pages 50-54

9

Charts on pages 52-54

Decorations with old-fashioned style are irresistible, whether it's a custom-framed Santa or softly stuffed adornments to trim your tree or packages. Projects such as these will strike a responsive chord with the child in every one of us.

Charts on pages 52-54

Chart on pages 50-51

13

Magnificent Story

The greatest and yet the simplest of stories, that of the Christ Child's birth, moves us as no other. The humble beginnings of the Prince of Peace have inspired artists and craftsmen throughout the centuries. The Victorians often turned to their needle and thread to retell the events of that miraculous night. We offer these eloquent samplers to help you create your own beautiful reminders of this magnificent story.

Charts on page 55

14

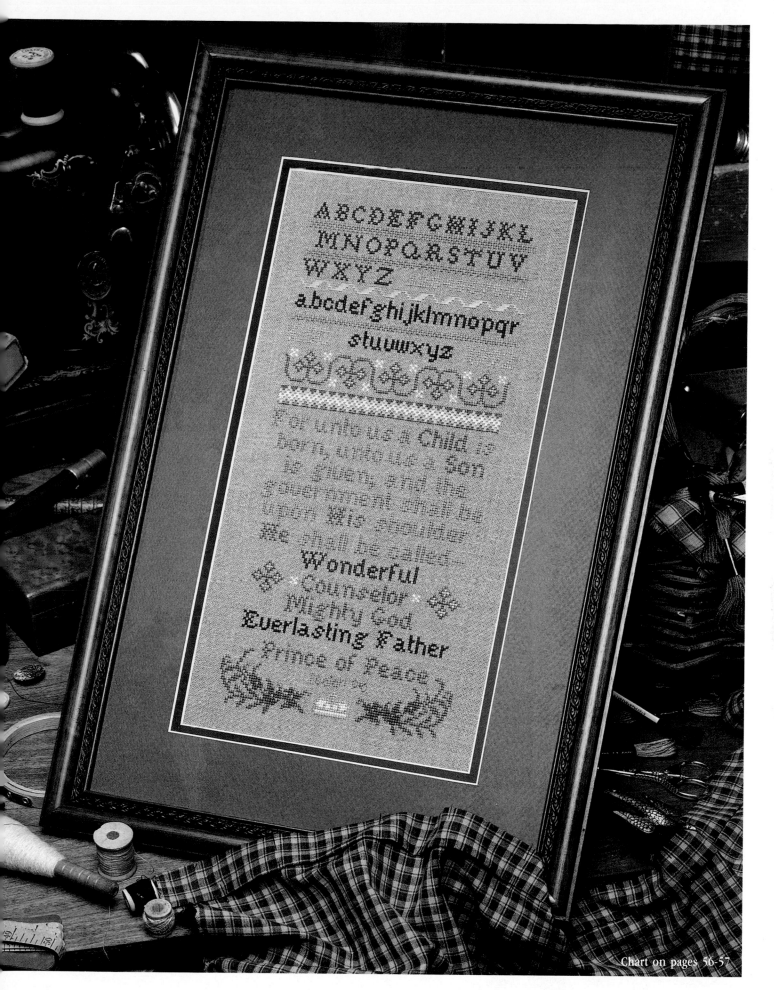

Chart on pages 56-57

Kittyland Christmas

It was a time when children invited their kittens to tea and even dressed them for the occasion. It was the Victorian Era, replete with feline fashion, fairy tales, and frippery. Illustrators gave us cats with human qualities, posing as teachers, opera singers, sailors, and acrobats. But the most important role in which dear Tabby appeared was that of doting mother and homemaker. She represented the genteel lady who tended her babies, tatted lace doilies, and spoke in measured tones on tasteful topics. These adorable kitten ornaments recall those sentimental days. Their sweet little faces and large liquid eyes will help you create a romantic, old-fashioned tree like one that could have graced your grandmother's sideboard.

Charts on pages 58-59

freedom's Jubilee

Proud and patriotic, turn-of-the-century Americans enjoyed coloring their Yuletide celebration red, white, and blue. It was their enthusiastic national spirit that led artists of that period to give us a truly American Santa Claus. Often, the jolly gift-giver was pictured like this one on his midnight flight o'er the land of the free.

Chart on pages 60-61

america has ever been a land of liberty and justice for all. Today, as our ancestors did a century ago, we take pride in choosing Christmas decorations that reflect our national heritage. Many Victorian trees were trimmed with miniature flags that waved amidst balls and beads and other trimmings of red, white, and blue. The angels and beaded ornament here combine the magic of Christmas with the jubilation of Independence Day to create a uniquely American collection.

Chart on page 63

Charts on pages 62-63

fanciful flower girls

Surrounding the innocence of a youthful face with delicate petals was a natural choice for the Victorians, who adored both children and flowers. Dainty little flower girls were often featured on postcards, scraps, and other keepsakes of this time. In this sentimental collection, these fanciful images from the past have been recreated as Christmas ornaments to adorn a tree or wreath.

Charts on page 86

St. Nicholas Remembered

Celebrated in olden times on December 6, St. Nicholas' Day signaled the beginning of the holiday season — a time for people to remember others and to give of themselves. The patron saint of children, St. Nicholas of Myra (now Turkey) was a fourth century bishop whose generosity was legendary. Gifts such as fruit and nuts were often exchanged on St. Nicholas' Eve in remembrance of his spirit of joyful giving.

Charts on pages 68-69

Snow Dreams of Yesteryear

A glistening carpet of new-fallen snow — this has been the Christmas wish of people everywhere throughout the years. Decades before Bing Crosby popularized the sentimental song about it, the Victorians were dreaming of a white Christmas. Their decorations were awash with white: Santa wore a long silvery beard and a coat of white fur; childlike angels were dressed in creamy robes; and doves the color of snow lent a pure and innocent feeling to cards and ornaments. To this generation of gentlefolk who aspired to a virtuous life, a clean white dusting from the heavens was an appropriate backdrop for a truly perfect Christmas.

Charts on pages 70-74

Charts on pages 74-75

Chart on pages 70-71

Charts on pages 72-75

toys from long ago

Through the years, stuffed toys have lived up to the grand expectations of children, serving as confidantes, best friends, and playmates. The advent of cuddly printed cloth toys in the late nineteenth century allowed more children than ever to forge new friendships with these special companions. Less expensive than ready-made dolls yet more sophisticated than those fashioned at home from wood, cornhusks, or scraps of cloth, the cut-and-sew patterns encountered widespread popularity. Adapted from these cherished toys of long ago, the tree ornaments here feature a few of our favorites: a lovable teddy, an adorable tabby, and a precious puppy.

Charts on pages 76-77

holy Night Nativity

O come, little children, O come one and all!
O come to the cradle in Bethlehem's stall!
Come, look in the manger! There sleeps on the hay
An infant so lovely, in light bright as day.

— CHRISTOPH VON SCHMID

Charts on pages 87-91

Bountiful
Christmastide

*During the holidays, the Christmas tree was the center of attention in every
Victorian parlor. Its branches were carefully decorated from top to bottom,
and fruit — sugared and gilded to dazzle the eyes — was often the finest of
all the trimmings. Honoring the importance of fruit as a traditional Christmas
treat, the designs at right are adapted from turn-of-the-century ornaments.
The handsome wreath pillow makes a lovely holiday accent.*

Chart on page 80

Charts on page 79

Santa's bag of gifts is always full of surprises, whether it's fruits and nuts or toy soldiers and dolls. The rosy-cheeked traveler here, wind-blown and chilled from his snowy trek, bears a bulging sack overflowing with a bountiful harvest of apples, walnuts, and other hidden goodies — favorite holiday treats in Victorian times.

Chart on pages 78-79

keepsake Confections

Chart on page 64

Around the turn of the century, concealing candy and other treats in artful containers was a popular custom at Christmastime. The clever holders, with their hidden treasures, were hung on the tree as delightful ornaments, placed on tabletops as charming decorations, or exchanged as small remembrances among friends. Limited only by the maker's imagination, they were fashioned from an assortment of materials into fanciful images in all shapes and sizes. Beloved symbols of the joyous Christmas season adorn the candy containers assembled here, lending a special touch to an old-fashioned Yuletide tradition.

Charts on pages 65-66

May
every joy
gladden
your
heart.

Charts on pages 64-66

holiday heritage

Embracing a rich history of cherished family traditions, Christmas celebrations strengthen our ties with one another. Memories of holidays past are recounted with pleasure as friends and relatives gather again to share the joy of the season. Photographs of loved ones who have joined in the festivities over the years will look charming in these old-fashioned frames. The other mementos will be sweet reminders of the love and laughter exchanged during Christmas.

Charts on pages 83-85

Chart on page 81

Sharing a bond of love and bright dreams for the future, a new couple's first Christmas together is a magical milestone. As two become three, the holiday season takes on an added dimension. Commemorating these important occasions, the lovely picture frames here are as special as the precious photographs they hold. Handmade ornaments, stitched with love today, will become tomorrow's keepsakes — to be passed along, with the family's holiday heritage, from one generation to the next.

Chart on page 84

Charts on page 82

Charts on page 83

Chart on page 85

The Christmas family party that we mean, is not a mere assembling of relations, got up at a week or two's notice, originating this year, having no family precedent in the last, and not likely to be repeated in the next. It is an annual gathering of all the accessible members of the family, young or old, rich or poor; and all the children look forward to it, for two months beforehand, in a fever of anticipation.

— CHARLES DICKENS

The Gracious Evergreen

O Christmas tree, O Christmas tree! With happiness we greet you.
When decked with candles once a year, You fill our hearts with Yuletide cheer.
O Christmas tree, O Christmas tree! With happiness we greet you.

O Christmas tree, O Christmas tree! How lovely are your branches.
In summer sun, in winter snow, A dress of green you always show.
O Christmas tree, O Christmas tree! How lovely are your branches.

— OLD CAROL

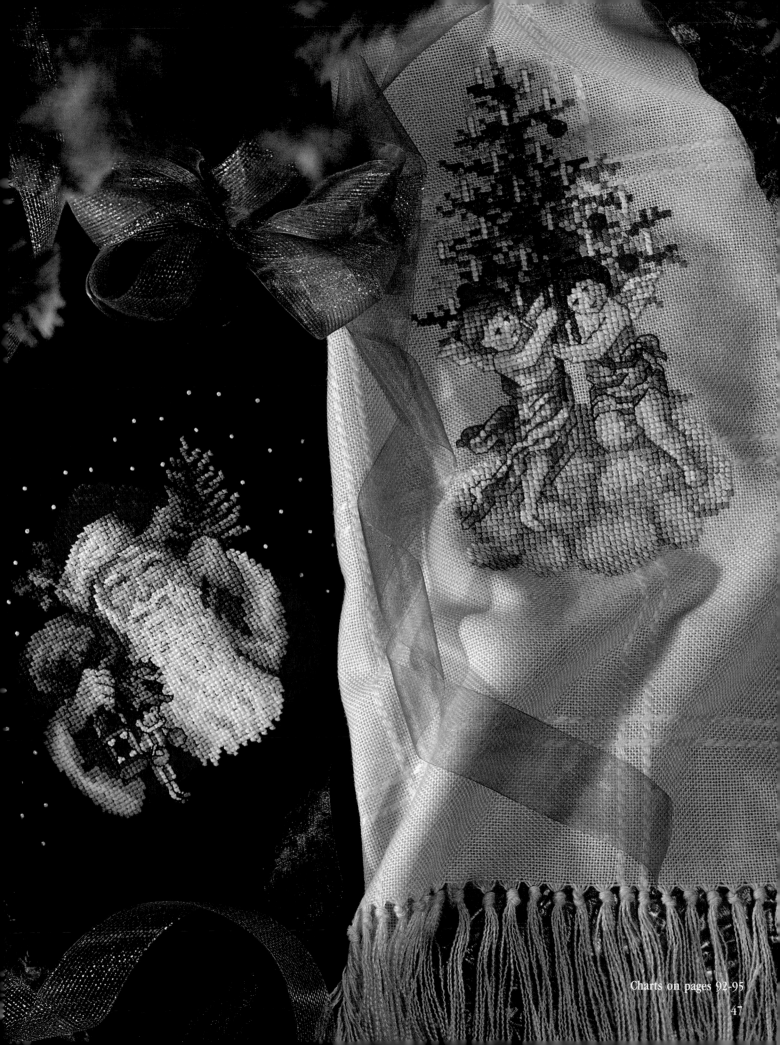

Charts on pages 92-95

O Christmas Tree

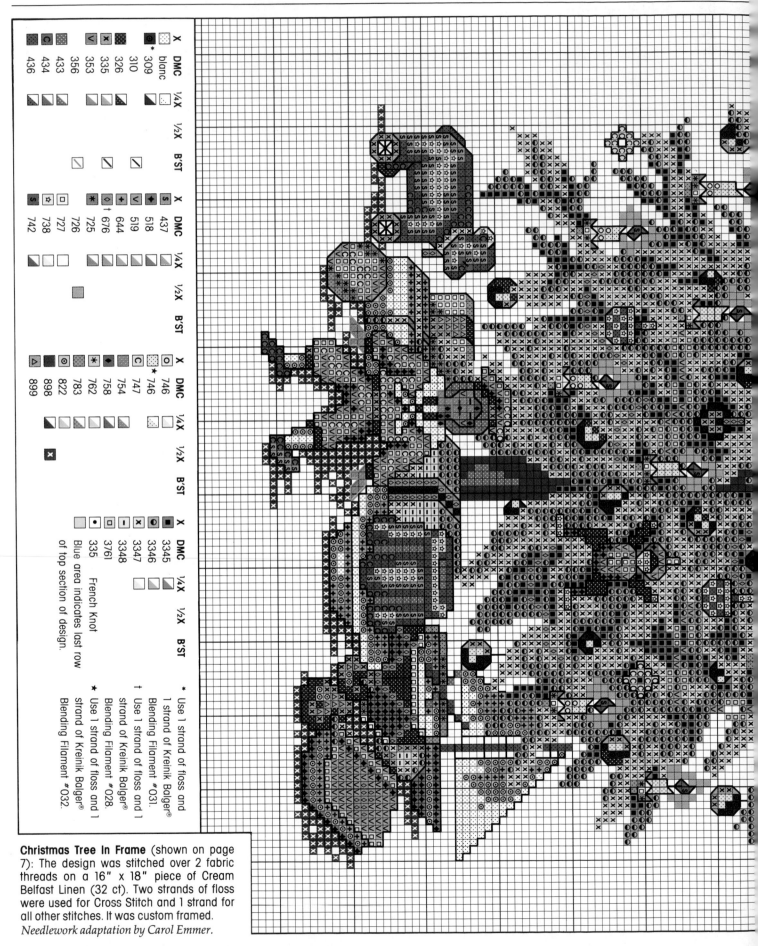

X							DMC	1/4X	1/2X	B'ST
							blanc			
							*309			
							310		�río	
							326			◥
							335			◥
							353			
							356			
							433			
							434			
							436			

X						S	X	DMC	1/4X	1/2X	B'ST
						S		437			
								518			
							V	519			
								644			
							†	676			
								725		◼	
								726			
						✿		727			
						▢		738			
								742			

△	◼	◉		✱	◆	C	O	X	DMC	1/4X	1/2X	B'ST
							★		746			
						C			747			
									754			
									758			
									762			
									783			
									822			
									898	◥		
									899			

	•	▢	I	X	◑	◼	X	DMC	1/4X	1/2X	B'ST
								3345			
								3346			
								3347			
								3348			
								3761			
								335	French Knot		

335 Blue area indicates last row of top section of design.

* Use 1 strand of floss and 1 strand of Kreinik Balger® Blending Filament #031.

† Use 1 strand of floss and 1 strand of Kreinik Balger® Blending Filament #028.

★ Use 1 strand of floss and 1 strand of Kreinik Balger® Blending Filament #032.

Christmas Tree In Frame (shown on page 7): The design was stitched over 2 fabric threads on a 16" x 18" piece of Cream Belfast Linen (32 ct). Two strands of floss were used for Cross Stitch and 1 strand for all other stitches. It was custom framed.
Needlework adaptation by Carol Emmer.

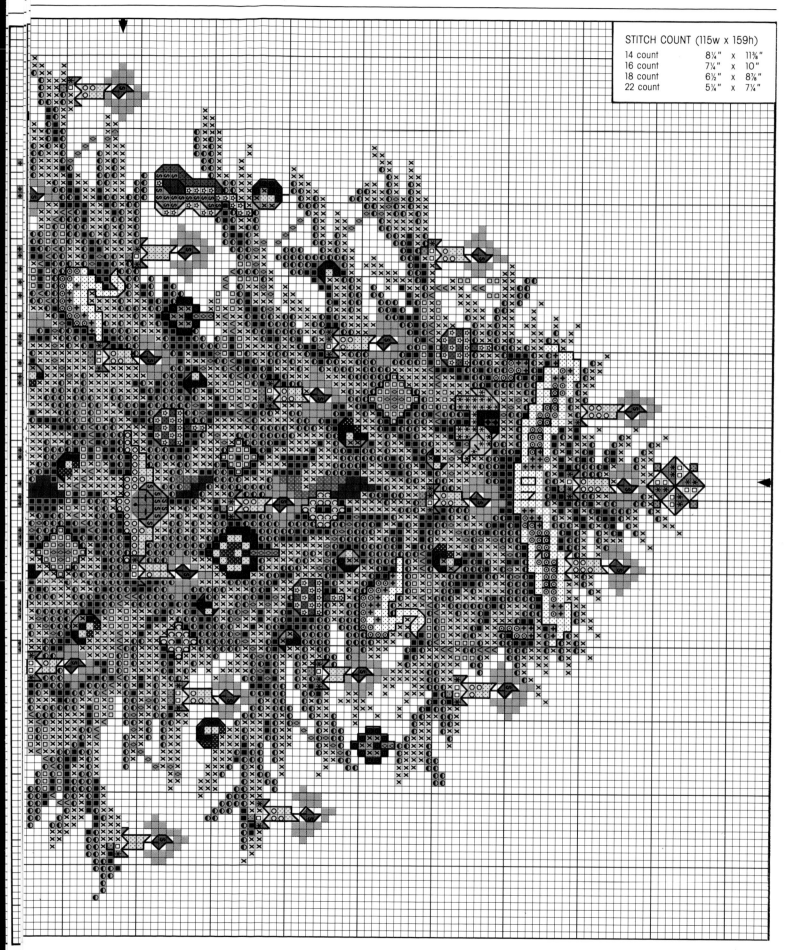

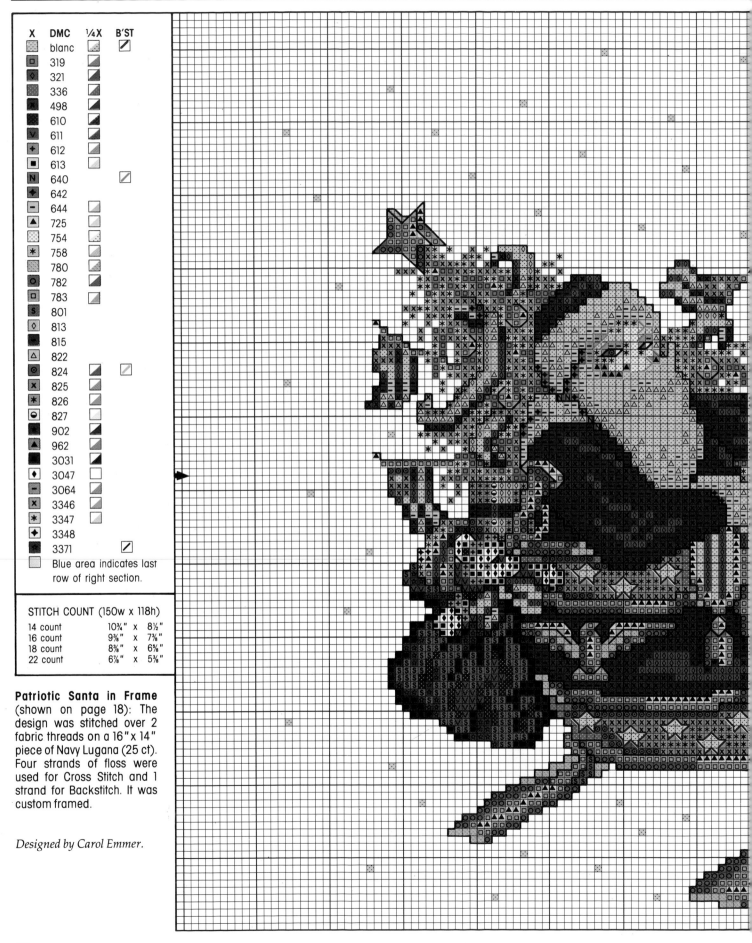

X	DMC	¼X	B'ST
	blanc		
	319		
	321		
	336		
	498		
	610		
	611		
	612		
	613		
N	640		
	642		
-	644		
▲	725		
	754		
*	758		
	780		
O	782		
	783		
S	801		
	813		
	815		
△	822		
G	824		
X	825		
*	826		
⊙	827		
	902		
▲	962		
	3031		
◆	3047		
-	3064		
X	3346		
*	3347		
◆	3348		
	3371		

Blue area indicates last row of right section.

STITCH COUNT (150w x 118h)

14 count	10¾"	x	8½"
16 count	9⅜"	x	7⅜"
18 count	8⅜"	x	6⅝"
22 count	6⅞"	x	5⅜"

Patriotic Santa in Frame (shown on page 18): The design was stitched over 2 fabric threads on a 16" x 14" piece of Navy Lugana (25 ct). Four strands of floss were used for Cross Stitch and 1 strand for Backstitch. It was custom framed.

Designed by Carol Emmer.

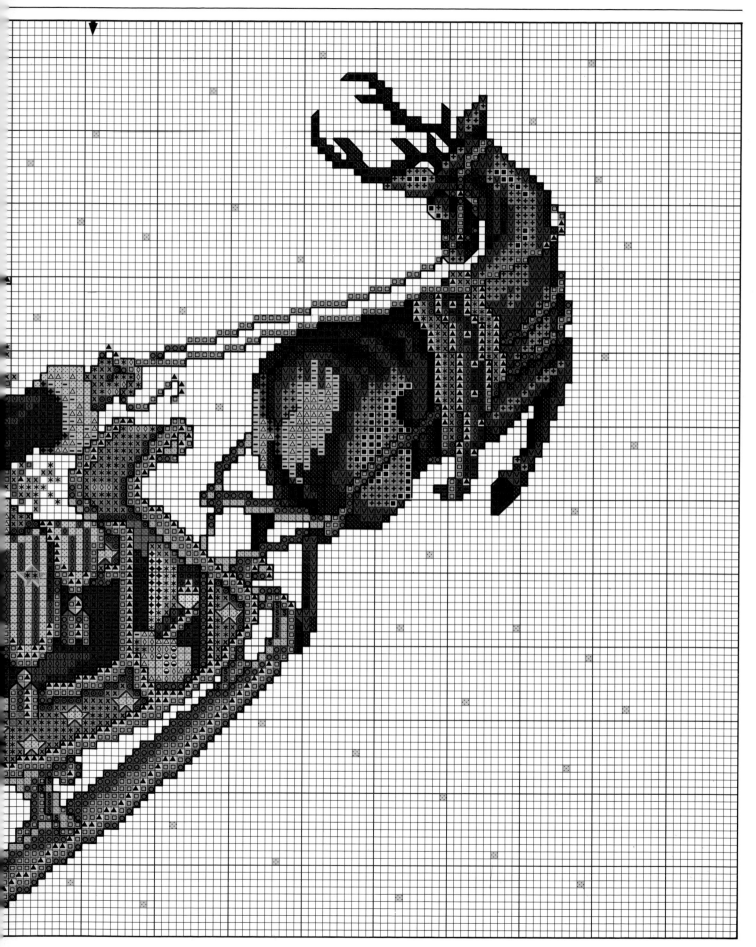

freedom's jubilee

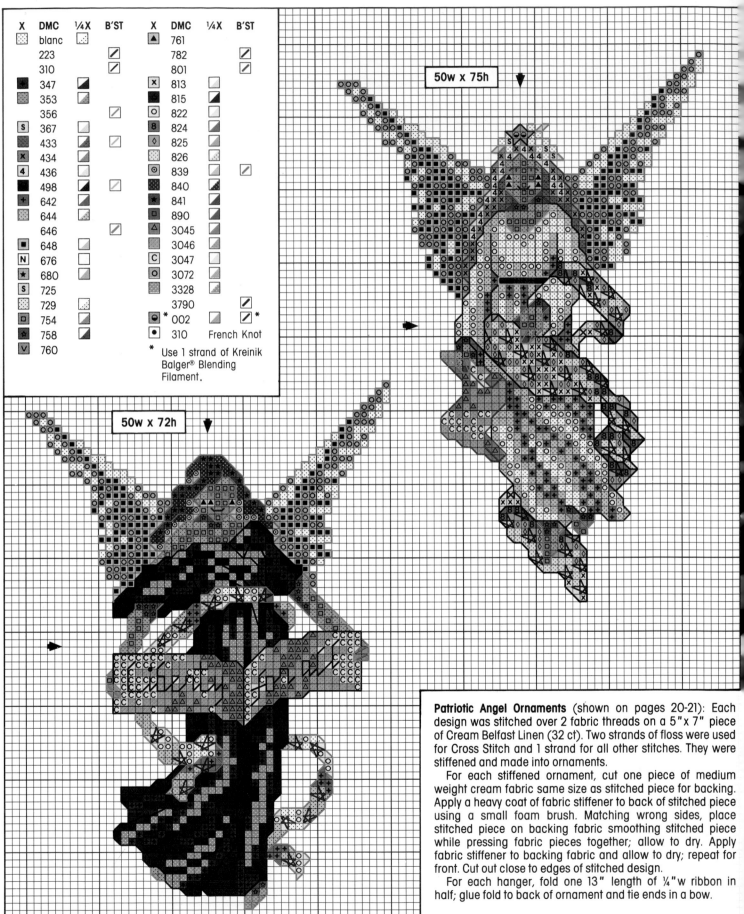

X	DMC	1/4X	B'ST	X	DMC	1/4X	B'ST
	blanc			▲	761		
	223		⁄		782		⁄
	310		⁄		801		⁄
✱	347	◣		X	813	◹	
	353	◹		■	815	◣	
	356		⁄	⊙	822		
S	367	◹	⁄	8	824	◹	
	433	◹	⁄	◊	825	◹	
X	434	◹			826	◹	
4	436	◹		⊙	839	◹	⁄
■	498	◣	⁄	■	840	◤	
✦	642	◹		★	841	◹	
	644	◹			890	◹	
	646		⁄	△	3045	◹	
■	648	◹			3046	◹	
N	676			C	3047	◹	
★	680	◹		O	3072	◹	
S	725	◹			3328	◹	
	729	◹			3790		⁄
◻	754	◹		⊖	002 *	◹	⁄ *
✿	758	◣		•	310		French Knot
V	760	◣					

* Use 1 strand of Kreinik
Balger® Blending
Filament.

50w x 75h

50w x 72h

Patriotic Angel Ornaments (shown on pages 20-21): Each
design was stitched over 2 fabric threads on a 5"x 7" piece
of Cream Belfast Linen (32 ct). Two strands of floss were used
for Cross Stitch and 1 strand for all other stitches. They were
stiffened and made into ornaments.

For each stiffened ornament, cut one piece of medium
weight cream fabric same size as stitched piece for backing.
Apply a heavy coat of fabric stiffener to back of stitched piece
using a small foam brush. Matching wrong sides, place
stitched piece on backing fabric smoothing stitched piece
while pressing fabric pieces together; allow to dry. Apply
fabric stiffener to backing fabric and allow to dry; repeat for
front. Cut out close to edges of stitched design.

For each hanger, fold one 13" length of ¼"w ribbon in
half; glue fold to back of ornament and tie ends in a bow.

Needlework adaptation by Jane Chandler.

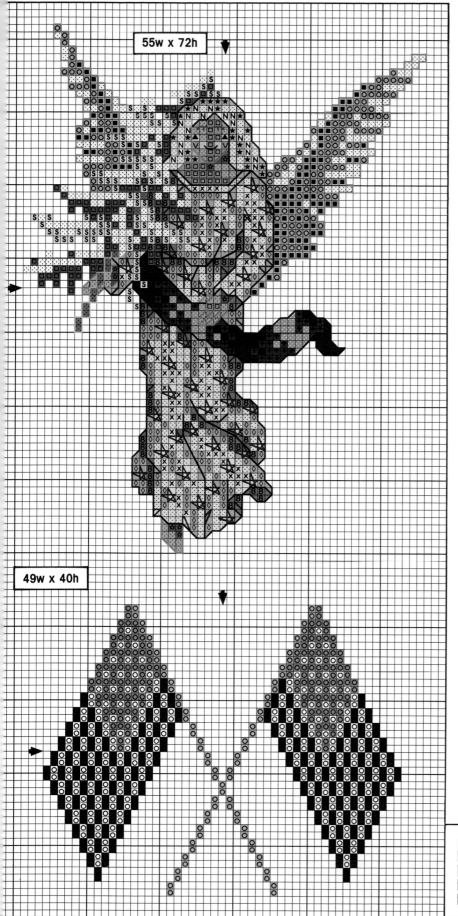

55w x 72h

49w x 40h

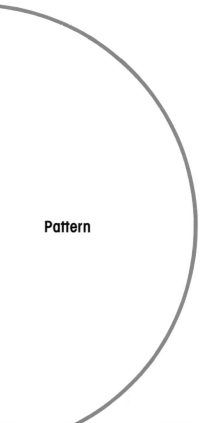

Pattern

Flag Beaded Ornament (shown on page 20): The design was worked over 2 fabric threads on a 9" square of Navy Lugana (25 ct). It was made into a stuffed ornament.

For attaching beads to fabric, refer to chart for bead placement and sew bead in place using sewing thread or nylon line and a fine needle that will pass through bead. Bring needle up through fabric, run needle through bead then down through fabric making a Half Cross Stitch as shown in **Fig. 1**, page 82. Secure thread on back or move to next bead.

For ornament, cut one 9" square of Lugana for backing. Matching right sides and raw edges, pin beaded design and backing fabric together. For pattern, fold sheet of tracing paper in half and place fold of paper on dashed line of pattern. Trace pattern onto tracing paper; cut out pattern. Unfold pattern and press flat. Center pattern on wrong side of beaded design and draw around pattern on fabric with fabric marking pencil. Sew fabric pieces together directly on drawn line leaving an opening for turning and stuffing. Trim excess fabric leaving ⅛" seam allowance. Turn right side out, stuff ornament with polyester fiberfill, and whipstitch opening closed. Beginning and ending at bottom of ornament, whipstitch one 17" length of ¼" dia. gold cord along seamline with nylon line; tack ends to back of ornament.

Designed by Jane Chandler.

MILL HILL BEADS	
00020	
00221	
00479	
00968	

keepsake Confections

Wreath and Bird Shaker Boxes
Instructions on page 67

Santa Pail
Instructions on page 67.

Wreath (59w x 59h)

Santa (31w x 41h)

Bird (57w x 54h)

X	DMC	¼X	B'ST	X	DMC	¼X	B'ST
	blanc				801		
	310				814		
	317				815		
	318				822		
	319				838		*
	320				890		†
	321				895		†
	347				898		*
	356				930		
	367				948		
	368				3064		
	371				3328		
	372				3347		
	413				3348		
	414				3712		
	415				3799		
	433				gold metallic		★
	469				blanc French Knot		
	471				310 French Knot		
	498						
	640						
	642						
	644						
	754						
	758						
	760						

* Use 838 for Santa. Use 898 for Bird.

† Use 890 for Wreath. Use 895 for Bird.

★ Use two strands of Kreinik Balger® Cable #002P.

64

Poinsettia and Holly Crackers
Instructions on page 66.

Poinsettia Cracker
(68w x 28h)

Holly Cracker
(68w x 28h)

Angel and Poinsettia Cones
Instructions on page 67.

Angel Cone (45w x 62h)

Poinsettia Cone (36w x 55h)

X	DMC	¼X	B'ST
	320		
	347		
	356		
	367		
-	368		
	369		
	433		*
	434		
	676		
	680		
	727		
	729		
	746		
	754		
S	758		
	760		
V	761		
	781		
	783		
	801		*
	814		†
	815		†
	839		*
	895		★
	924		♦
	926		
X	927		
C	928		
	930		
	986		★
	987		
*	989		
	3064		
	3328		
	3345		
	3346		
S	3347		
O	3348		
	3768		♦
	3779		

* Use 433 for Angel Cone. Use 801 for Poinsettia and Holly Crackers. Use 839 for Poinsettia Cone.

† Use 814 for Poinsettia and Holly Crackers. Use 815 for Poinsettia Cone.

★ Use 895 for Holly Cracker and Poinsettia Cone. Use 986 for Poinsettia Cracker.

♦ Use 924 for Poinsettia Cone. Use 3768 for Angel Cone.

St. Nicholas Remembered

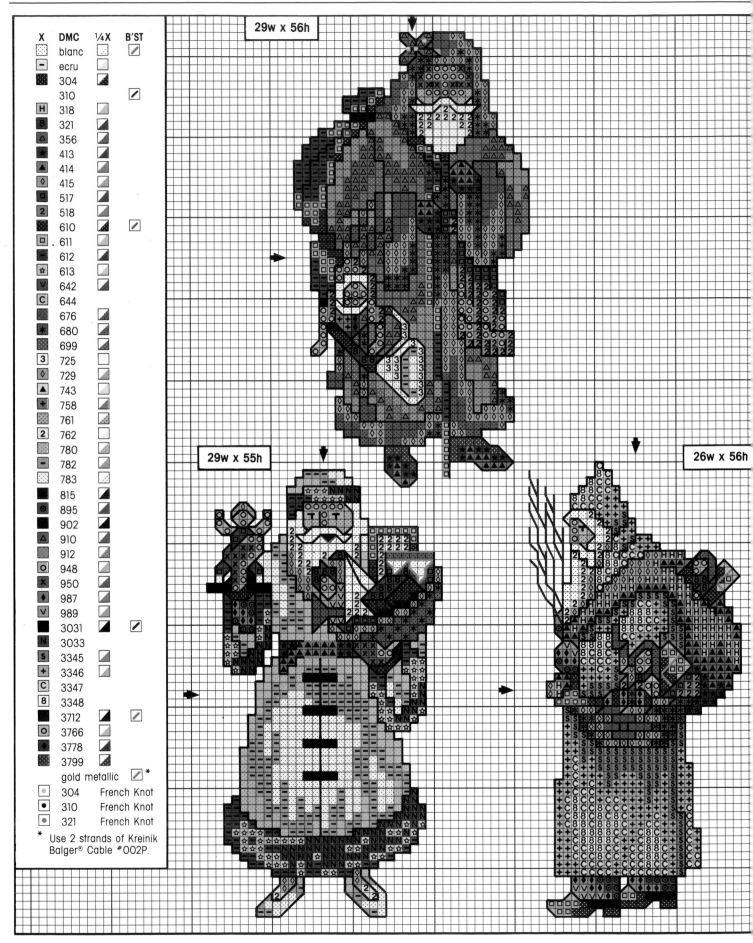

X	DMC	¼X	B'ST
	blanc		/
-	ecru		
	304	/	
	310		/
H	318		
8	321	/	
△	356		
★	413	/	
▲	414	/	
◇	415	/	
□	517	/	
2	518	/	
	610	/	/
□	611		
-	612	/	
☆	613	/	
V	642		
C	644		
	676	/	
✳	680	/	
	699	/	
3	725		
◇	729	/	
▲	743		
+	758		
	761	/	
2	762		
	780	/	
-	782	/	
	783		
	815	/	
⊙	895	/	
	902	/	
△	910	/	
	912	/	
O	948	/	
✳	950	/	
◆	987	/	
V	989	/	
	3031	/	/
N	3033		
S	3345	/	
+	3346	/	
C	3347		
8	3348		
	3712	/	/
O	3766	/	
✳	3778	/	
	3799	/	
	gold metallic	/	*
◦	304	French Knot	
●	310	French Knot	
◉	321	French Knot	

* Use 2 strands of Kreinik Balger® Cable #002P.

29w x 56h

29w x 55h

26w x 56h

38w x 57h

30w x 61h

38w x 59h

St. Nicholas Ornaments (shown on pages 24-25): Each design was stitched over 2 fabric threads on a 6" x 8" piece of Natural Irish Linen (36 ct). Two strands of floss were used for Cross Stitch and 1 strand for all other stitches. They were made into fringed ornaments.

For each ornament, trim stitched piece ¾" larger than design on all sides. Cut a piece of Irish Linen same size as stitched piece for backing. With wrong sides facing, use desired floss color to cross stitch fabric pieces together ¼" from bottom and side edges. Stuff with polyester fiberfill. Cross stitch across top of ornament ¼" from edge. Fringe fabric to cross-stitched lines.

For each hanger, fold one 5" length of jute in half; whipstitch ends to back of ornament.

Needlework adaptation by Nancy Dockter.

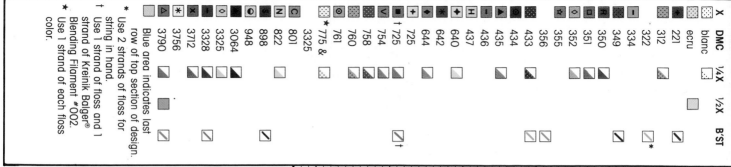

The chart legend lists the following DMC floss colors with their symbols (columns: X, ¼X, ½X, B'ST, DMC):

blanc, ecru, 221, 312, 322, 334, 349, 350, 351, 352, 355, 356, 433, 434, 435, 436, 437, 640, 642, 644, 725, 725, 754, 758, 760, 761, 775 &, 3325, 801, 822, 898, 948, 3064, 3325, 3328, 3712, 3756, 3790

Legend notes:
- Blue area indicates last row of top section of design.
- ★ Use 2 strands of floss for string in hand.
- † Use 1 strand of floss and 1 strand of Kreinik Balger® Blending Filament #002.
- ✳ Use 1 strand of each floss color.

White Santa In Frame (shown on page 26): The design was stitched over 2 fabric threads on a 10" x 14" piece of Raw Belfast Linen (32 ct). Two strands of floss were used for Cross Stitch and 1 strand for Backstitch. It was custom framed.

White Santa Treetop Ornament (shown on page 30): The design was stitched over 2 fabric threads on a 10" x 14" piece of Raw Belfast Linen (32 ct). Two strands of floss were used for Cross Stitch and 1 strand for Backstitch. It was made into a treetop ornament.

For treetop ornament, cut one piece of Belfast Linen same size as stitched piece for backing. For pattern, lay stitched piece on flat surface and place tracing paper over stitched piece. Referring to **Fig. 1** for shape, draw pattern 1½" larger than design on all sides; cut out pattern. Matching right sides and raw edges, pin stitched piece and backing fabric together. Center pattern on wrong side of stitched piece and use a fabric marking pencil to draw around pattern. Cut fabric pieces along drawn line; remove pins.

Cut one 28" length of purchased ¼" dia. cording. If needed, trim seam allowance of cording to ½". Matching raw edges and beginning and ending at bottom edge of stitched piece, baste cording to right side of stitched piece.

Matching right sides and raw edges and leaving bottom edge open, use a zipper foot and ½" seam allowance to sew stitched piece and backing fabric together. Clip curves and turn right side out, carefully pushing curves outward. Press bottom edge ½" to wrong side. Stuff with polyester fiberfill and whipstitch bottom edge closed.

For ties, cut two 18" lengths of ¼"w ribbon. Fold each length in half and whipstitch center of each length to back of treetop ornament 4" apart (**Fig. 2**).

Needlework adaptation by Carol Emmer.

Fig. 1

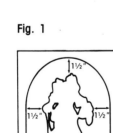

Fig. 2

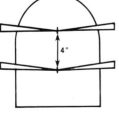

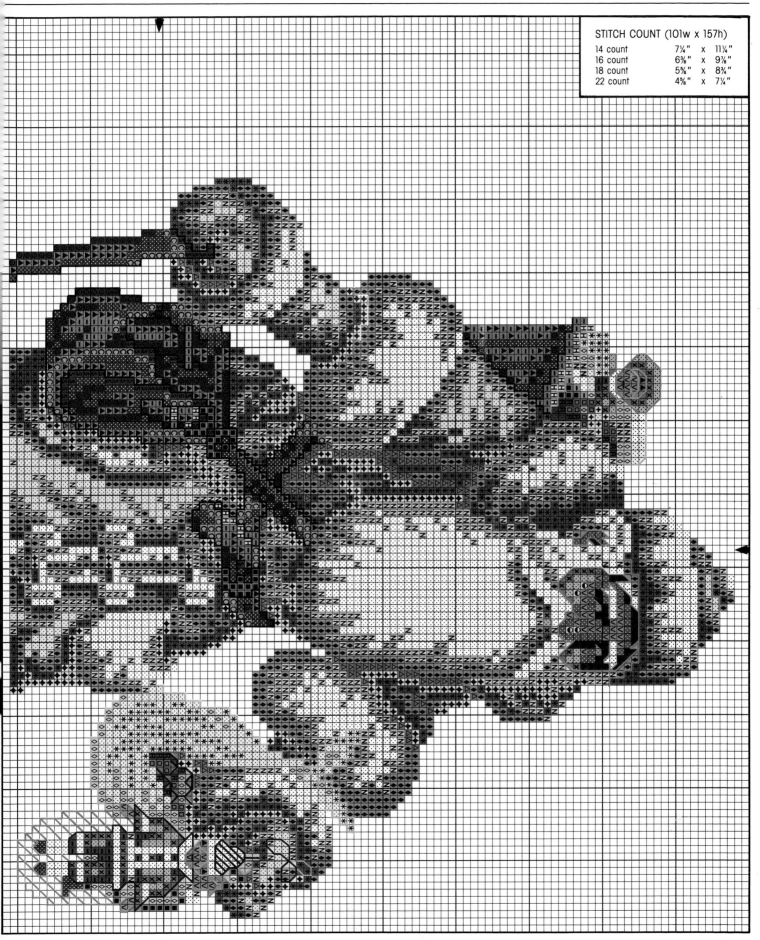

STITCH COUNT (101w x 157h)		
14 count	7¼"	x	11¼"
16 count	6⅜"	x	9⅞"
18 count	5⅝"	x	8¾"
22 count	4⅝"	x	7¼"

Snow Dreams of Yesteryear

Stitch Key
1 – Satin Stitch
2 – Padded Satin Stitch
3 – Buttonhole Stitch
4 – Backstitch
5 – Padded Fishbone Stitcn
6 – French Knot

Embroidered Tree Skirt (shown on page 31): The design was embroidered on a 30"x 15" piece of linen. Three strands of ecru embroidery floss were used for all stitches. It was made into a tree skirt.

For tree skirt, you will need 1½ yds of 45"w linen for border, 2¼ yds of 60"w desired fabric for tree skirt, 2¼ yds of 60"w fabric for lining, 5¼ yds of ½" dia. purchased cording, thread to match fabric, 1 yd of string, thumbtack, pencil, tracing paper, hot-iron transfer pencil, glue, craft paper, and a fabric marking pencil.

For transferring design to fabric, glue pieces of tracing paper together to make a 25"x 11" piece of tracing paper. Matching short edges, fold paper in half and place fold on dashed line of pattern; trace design with a hot-iron transfer pencil matching arrows of pattern to form one design. **Do not trace instructional markings or arrows.** Turn tracing paper over and draw reverse design along traced lines with hot-iron transfer pencil. Unfold tracing paper.

Follow manufacturer's instructions to transfer design onto a 30"x 15" piece of linen. Embroider design following Stitch Key, Embroidery Stitch Diagrams, and instructional markings on chart.

For border pattern, glue pieces of tracing paper together to form one

25"x 11" piece of tracing paper. Matching short edges, fold paper in half and place fold along dashed line of pattern; trace pattern (indicated by blue lines on chart) onto paper matching arrows to form one pattern. Cut out pattern; unfold and press flat.

Center border pattern on right side of embroidered piece; pin in place. Draw around pattern using fabric marking pencil; cut out. Repeat with remaining linen for a total of eight pieces.

For tree skirt pattern, cut one 22" square of craft paper; place on flat surface. To mark outer cutting line, tie one end of string to pencil. Insert thumbtack through string 22" from pencil. Referring to **Fig. 1**, page 50, insert thumbtack and mark one-fourth of a circle. To mark inner cutting line on pattern, insert thumbtack through string 1½" from pencil and mark one-fourth of a circle. Cut out pattern and fold pattern in half to make one-eighth of a circle. Cut pattern along fold from outer edge to inner edge.

Place one-eighth circle pattern on tree skirt fabric; pin in place. Draw around pattern using fabric marking pencil; cut out. Repeat for a total of eight pieces.

Matching right sides and raw edges, use a ½" seam allowance to

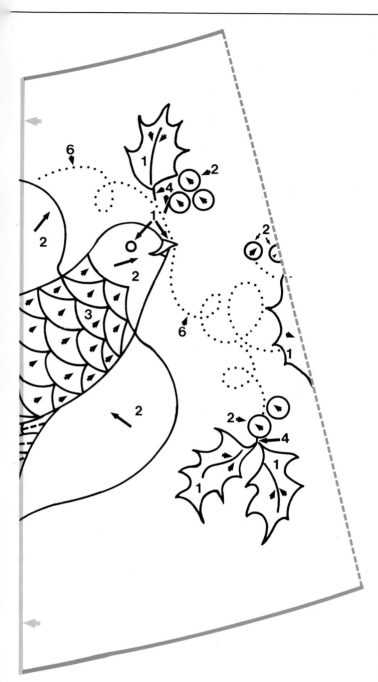

EMBROIDERY STITCH DIAGRAMS

Satin Stitch: Following **Fig. 1**, come up at odd numbers and go down at even numbers with the stitches touching but not overlapping.

Fig. 1

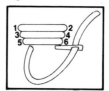

Padded Satin Stitch: (**Note:** Arrow in design indicates direction to stitch top layer.) Work a pad layer of Satin Stitch in direction opposite of arrow. Work second layer of Satin Stitch in direction of arrow over pad layer as shown in **Fig. 2**.

Fig. 2

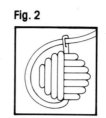

Buttonhole Stitch: Bring needle up at 1; go down at 2 and back up at 3 with needle on top of floss (**Fig. 3**). Work stitches close together but not overlapping (**Fig. 4**).

Fig. 3   **Fig. 4**

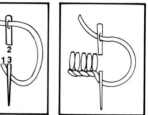

Stem Stitch: Following **Fig. 5**, come up at 1. Keeping the thread below the stitching line, go down at 2 and come up at 3. Go down at 4 and come up at 5.

Fig. 5

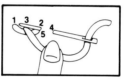

Backstitch: Bring needle up at 1; go down at 2 and come up at 3. Go down at 1 and come up at 4. Go down at 3 and come up at 5 (**Fig. 6**).

Fig. 6

Padded Fishbone Stitch: Work a pad layer of Satin Stitch covering design area. Following **Fig. 7**, bring needle up at 1 and go down diagonally with needle slightly overlapping center line. Come up at 2 and go down diagonally with needle slightly overlapping center line. Repeat, alternating sides as indicated by numbers.

Fig. 7

French Knot: Bring needle up at 1. Wrap floss once around needle and insert needle at 2, holding end of floss with non-stitching fingers (**Fig. 8**). Tighten knot; then pull needle through fabric, holding floss until it must be released.

Fig. 8

sew outside curved edge of one tree skirt piece to inside curved edge of one border piece; clip curves and press seam allowances open. Repeat with remaining pieces.

Matching right sides and raw edges, use ½" seam allowance to sew long edges of tree skirt pieces together; press seam allowances open.

For opening in back of skirt, fold in half tree skirt piece opposite embroidered piece. Cut along fold from outer edge to inner edge.

If needed, trim seam allowance of ½" dia. cording to ½". With beginning and end of cording extending 1" past edges of back opening, match right sides and raw edges and baste cording to border of tree skirt. Use zipper foot to sew cording to border of tree skirt using a ½" seam allowance.

For lining, match right sides of tree skirt and lining fabric; pin in place. Using tree skirt as pattern, cut lining fabric even with edges of tree skirt. Using a ½" seam allowance and zipper foot, sew fabric pieces together leaving one straight edge open; clip curves. Turn tree skirt right side out and press. Sew final closure by hand.

Designed by Diane Brakefield.

Snow Dreams of Yesteryear

Stitch Key
1 — Satin Stitch
2 — Padded Satin Stitch
3 — Buttonhole Stitch
4 — Stem Stitch
5 — Backstitch
6A — French Knot (3 strands)
6B — French Knot (5 strands)

Embroidered Ornaments (shown on pages 26-31): Each design was embroidered on an 8" x 7" piece of linen. Three strands of ecru embroidery floss were used for all stitches unless otherwise noted in Stitch Key. They were made into heart-shaped ornaments.

For each ornament, you will need tracing paper, pencil, one 8" x 7" piece of linen for backing, one 10" x 5" piece of adhesive board, one 10" x 5" piece of batting, one 14" length of ½"w flat lace, clear-drying craft glue, and a hot-iron transfer pencil.

To transfer each design, place piece of tracing paper over design; use pencil to trace design. **Do not trace instructional markings.** Turn tracing paper over and draw over traced lines with hot-iron transfer pencil. Follow manufacturer's instructions for transferring design onto 8" x 7" piece of linen. Embroider design following Stitch Key, Embroidery Stitch Diagrams, page 73, and instructional markings on chart.

For each heart pattern, fold tracing paper in half and place fold on dashed line of pattern; trace pattern onto tracing paper. Cut out each pattern; unfold patterns and press flat. Draw around small heart pattern twice on adhesive board and twice on batting; cut out shapes. Remove paper backing from each adhesive board piece and press one batting piece onto each adhesive board piece.

Center large heart pattern over embroidered piece and draw around pattern; cut out embroidered piece. Cut backing fabric same size as embroidered piece.

For ornament front, clip ⅜" into edges of embroidered piece at ½" intervals. Center embroidered piece over batting side of one adhesive board piece; turn edges to wrong side and glue in place. Repeat with backing fabric and remaining adhesive board piece for ornament back.

Beginning and ending at bottom of front piece; glue lace to wrong side of front piece. Glue wrong sides of ornament front and back together.

Designed by Diane Brakefield.

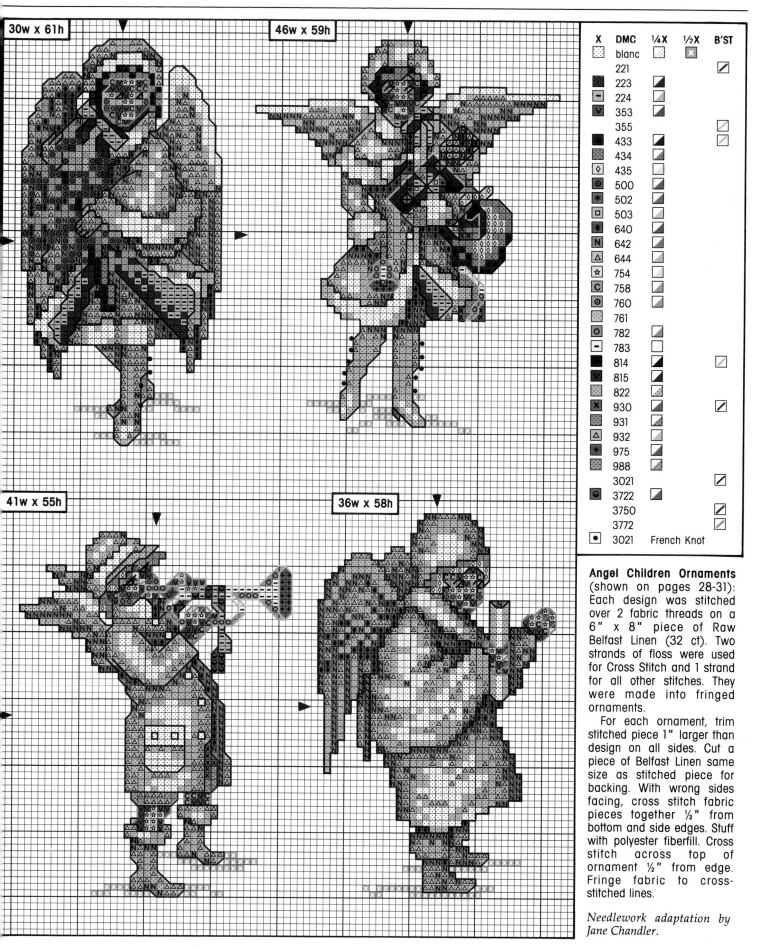

30w x 61h

46w x 59h

41w x 55h

36w x 58h

X	DMC	¼X	½X	B'ST
	blanc			
	221			
	223			
-	224			
V	353			
	355			
	433			
	434			
◇	435			
⊙	500			
✳	502			
⊡	503			
◆	640			
N	642			
△	644			
☆	754			
C	758			
⊙	760			
	761			
O	782			
-	783			
	814			
V	815			
	822			
✕	930			
	931			
△	932			
✚	975			
	988			
	3021			
⊙	3722			
	3750			
	3772			
●	3021	French Knot		

Angel Children Ornaments (shown on pages 28-31): Each design was stitched over 2 fabric threads on a 6" x 8" piece of Raw Belfast Linen (32 ct). Two strands of floss were used for Cross Stitch and 1 strand for all other stitches. They were made into fringed ornaments.

For each ornament, trim stitched piece 1" larger than design on all sides. Cut a piece of Belfast Linen same size as stitched piece for backing. With wrong sides facing, cross stitch fabric pieces together ½" from bottom and side edges. Stuff with polyester fiberfill. Cross stitch across top of ornament ½" from edge. Fringe fabric to cross-stitched lines.

Needlework adaptation by Jane Chandler.

75

toys from long ago

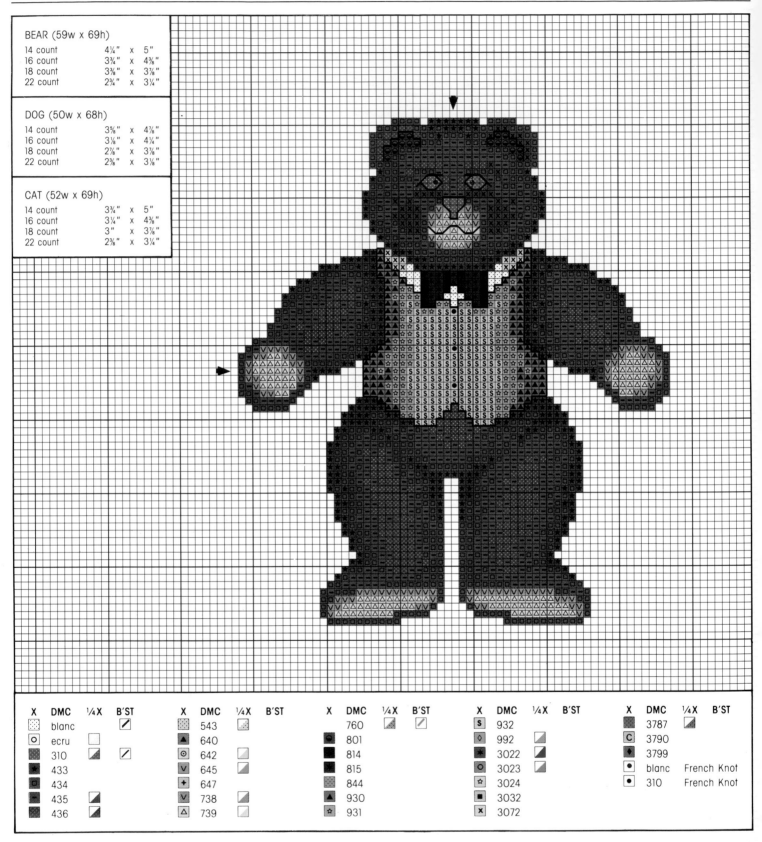

	BEAR (59w x 69h)		
	14 count	4¼"	x 5"
	16 count	3¾"	x 4⅜"
	18 count	3⅜"	x 3⅞"
	22 count	2¾"	x 3¼"

	DOG (50w x 68h)		
	14 count	3⅝"	x 4⅞"
	16 count	3⅛"	x 4¼"
	18 count	2⅞"	x 3¾"
	22 count	2⅜"	x 3⅛"

	CAT (52w x 69h)		
	14 count	3¾"	x 5"
	16 count	3¼"	x 4⅜"
	18 count	3"	x 3⅞"
	22 count	2⅜"	x 3¼"

X	DMC	¼X	B'ST	X	DMC	¼X	B'ST	X	DMC	¼X	B'ST	X	DMC	¼X	B'ST	X	DMC	¼X	B'ST
	blanc		◢		543	◢			760	◢	◢	S	932				3787	◢	
○	ecru	☐		▲	640			◉	801			◇	992	◢		C	3790		
	310	◢	◢	⊙	642	◢			814			✳	3022	◢		◆	3799		
★	433			V	645	◢			815			○	3023	◢		●	blanc		French Knot
▣	434			✚	647				844			☆	3024			●	310		French Knot
▨	435	◢		V	738	◢		▲	930			■	3032						
	436	◢		△	739	◢		☆	931			✕	3072						

Bear, Dog, and Cat Stuffed Shapes (shown on page 32): Each design was stitched on a 9" square of Ivory Aida (14 ct). Three strands of floss were used for Cross Stitch and 1 strand for all other stitches. They were made into stuffed shapes.

For each stuffed shape, trim stitched piece 1" larger than design on all sides. Cut a piece of Aida the same size as stitched piece for backing.

Matching right sides and raw edges and leaving an opening for turning and stuffing, sew stitched piece and backing fabric together ¼" from design. Trim excess fabric leaving a ¼" seam allowance. Trim corners, clip curves, and turn right side out. Stuff shape with polyester fiberfill and sew final closure by hand.

Needlework adaptation by Jane Chandler.

Bountiful Christmastide

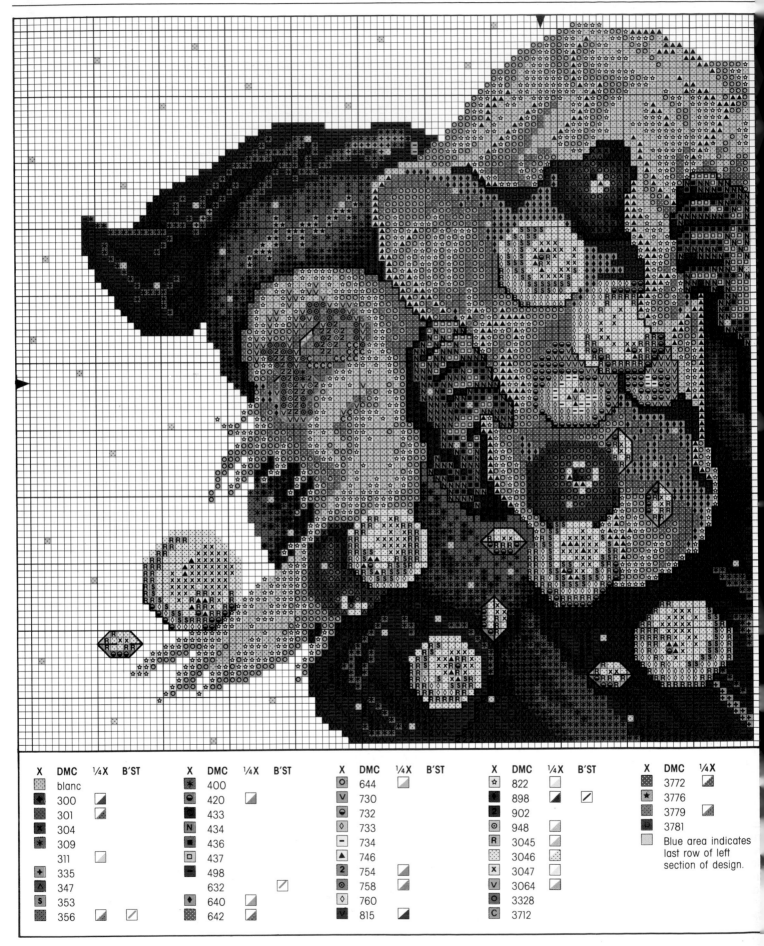

X	DMC	¼X	B'ST		X	DMC	¼X	B'ST		X	DMC	¼X	B'ST		X	DMC	¼X	B'ST		X	DMC	¼X
	blanc				✳	400				○	644	◩			☆	822	◩				3772	◩
◆	300	◢			◓	420	◢			V	730				◼	898	◥	◿		★	3776	
◼	301	◢				433				◒	732				2	902					3779	◩
✦	304				N	434				◇	733				◉	948	◩			▨	3781	
✳	309				◼	436				−	734				R	3045	◩					
	311	◩			▢	437				▲	746				▒	3046	▨			Blue area indicates		
✚	335				▬	498				2	754	◩			X	3047	◻			last row of left		
▲	347					632		◪		◎	758	◩			V	3064	◩			section of design.		
S	353				◆	640	◪			◇	760	◩			◉	3328	◩					
▨	356	◪	◪		▬	642	◪			V	815	◪			C	3712						

78

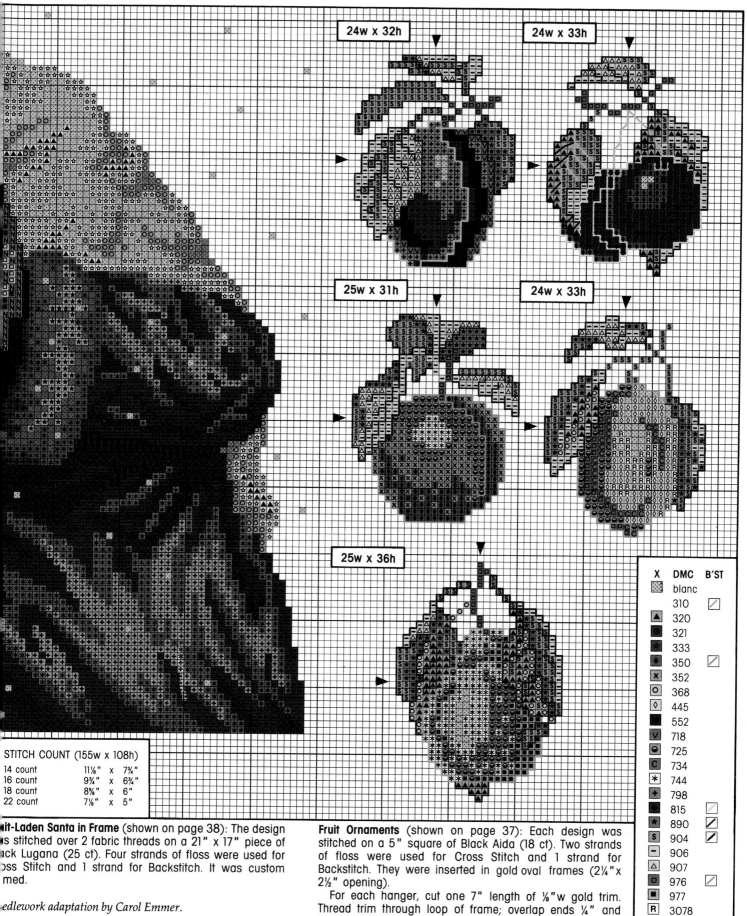

24w x 32h

24w x 33h

25w x 31h

24w x 33h

25w x 36h

STITCH COUNT (155w x 108h)

14 count	11⅛" x	7¾"
16 count	9¾" x	6¾"
18 count	8⅝" x	6"
22 count	7⅛" x	5"

X	DMC	B'ST
▨	blanc	
	310	╱
▲	320	
◉	321	
✶	333	
◆	350	╱
✕	352	
○	368	
◇	445	
▨	552	
▼	718	
◒	725	
◖	734	
✳	744	
✚	798	
■	815	╱
★	890	╱
S	904	╱
—	906	
△	907	
▢	976	╱
▣	977	
R	3078	

Fruit-Laden Santa in Frame (shown on page 38): The design was stitched over 2 fabric threads on a 21" x 17" piece of Black Lugana (25 ct). Four strands of floss were used for Cross Stitch and 1 strand for Backstitch. It was custom framed.

Needlework adaptation by Carol Emmer.

Fruit Ornaments (shown on page 37): Each design was stitched on a 5" square of Black Aida (18 ct). Two strands of floss were used for Cross Stitch and 1 strand for Backstitch. They were inserted in gold oval frames (2¼" x 2½" opening).

For each hanger, cut one 7" length of ⅛"w gold trim. Thread trim through loop of frame; overlap ends ¼" and glue in place.

Bountiful Christmastide

STITCH COUNT (90w x 90h)

14 count	6½"	x	6½"
16 count	5⅝"	x	5⅝"
18 count	5"	x	5"
22 count	4⅛"	x	4⅛"

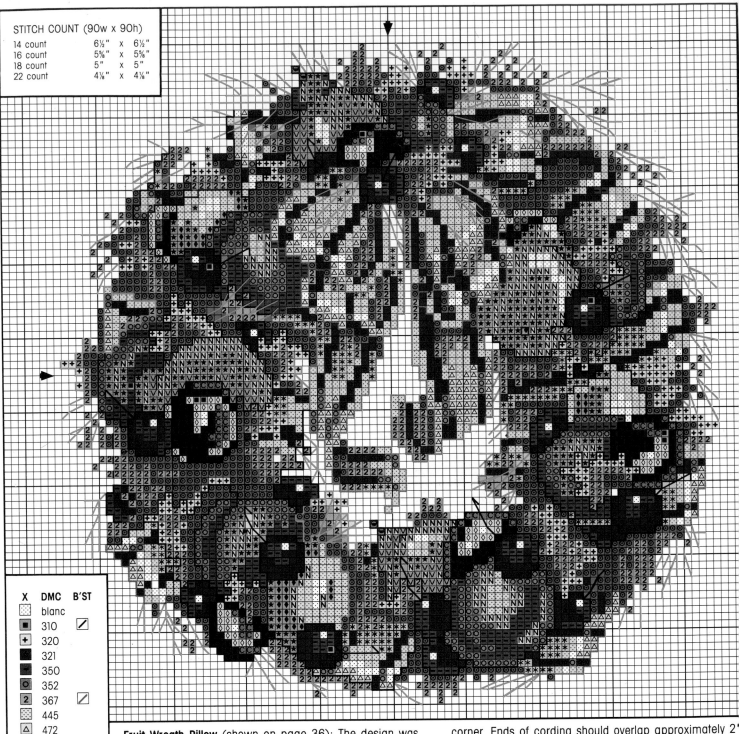

X	DMC	B'ST
⬚	blanc	
■	310	╱
✚	320	
◼	321	
◧	350	
◎	352	
2	367	╱
⬚	445	
△	472	
◼	552	
C	718	
★	725	
◆	734	
N	744	
◇	798	
◼	815	
⊙	890	╱
✱	906	
⬚	907	
◉	975	╱
V	977	

Fruit Wreath Pillow (shown on page 36): The design was stitched over 2 fabric threads on a 16" square of Black Lugana (25 ct). Four strands of floss were used for Cross Stitch and 1 strand for Backstitch (work DMC 890 branches in long stitches). It was made into a pillow.

For pillow, cut stitched piece 2" larger than design on all sides. Cut one piece of Lugana same size as stitched piece for backing.

For cording, cut one 4" x 46" bias strip of coordinating fabric. Center 1" dia. cord on wrong side of bias strip; matching long edges, fold strip over cord. Using zipper foot, baste along length of strip close to cord; trim seam allowance to ½". Matching raw edges and beginning at bottom center, pin cording to right side of stitched piece making a ⅜" clip in seam allowance of cording at each corner. Ends of cording should overlap approximately 2" pin overlapping end out of the way. Starting 2" from beginning end of cording and ending 4" from overlapping end, baste cording to stitched piece. On overlapping end cording, remove 2½" of basting; fold end of fabric back and trim cord so that it meets beginning end of cord. Fo end of fabric under ½"; wrap fabric over beginning end cording. Finish basting cording to stitched piece.

Matching right sides and raw edges, use a ½" sea allowance to sew stitched piece and backing fabric togeth leaving an opening for turning and stuffing. Trim sea allowances diagonally at corners and turn pillow right si out, carefully pushing corners outward. Stuff pillow wi polyester fiberfill and whipstitch opening closed.

Fruit Ornaments and Fruit Wreath Pillow designed Barbara Baatz of Kooler Design Studio.

X	DMC	B'ST
⊙	520	◪
+	522	
△	523	
▨	772	
◆	3350	
▲	3354	
2	3363	◪
	3685	◪
◎	3731	
C	3733	

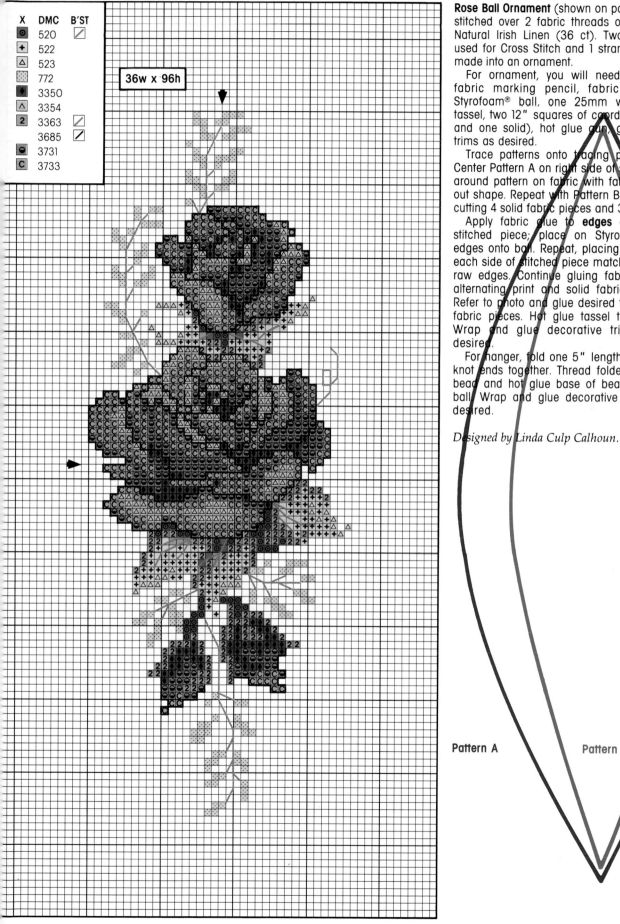

36w x 96h

Rose Ball Ornament (shown on page 43): The design was stitched over 2 fabric threads on a 6" x 12" piece of Natural Irish Linen (36 ct). Two strands of floss were used for Cross Stitch and 1 strand for Backstitch. It was made into an ornament.

For ornament, you will need tracing paper, pencil, fabric marking pencil, fabric glue, one 5½" dia. Styrofoam® ball, one 25mm wooden bead, one 6" tassel, two 12" squares of coordinating fabric (one print and one solid), hot glue gun, glue sticks, and various trims as desired.

Trace patterns onto tracing paper; cut out patterns. Center Pattern A on right side of stitched piece and draw around pattern on fabric with fabric marking pencil; cut out shape. Repeat with Pattern B on coordinating fabrics cutting 4 solid fabric pieces and 3 print fabric pieces.

Apply fabric glue to **edges only** of wrong side of stitched piece; place on Styrofoam® ball and press edges onto ball. Repeat, placing a solid fabric piece on each side of stitched piece matching points and aligning raw edges. Continue gluing fabric pieces around ball, alternating print and solid fabric pieces; allow to dry. Refer to photo and glue desired trims over raw edges of fabric pieces. Hot glue tassel to bottom of ornament. Wrap and glue decorative trims around tassel as desired.

For hanger, fold one 5" length of desired trim in half; knot ends together. Thread folded end through wooden bead and hot glue base of bead to top of Styrofoam® ball. Wrap and glue decorative trims around bead as desired.

Designed by Linda Culp Calhoun.

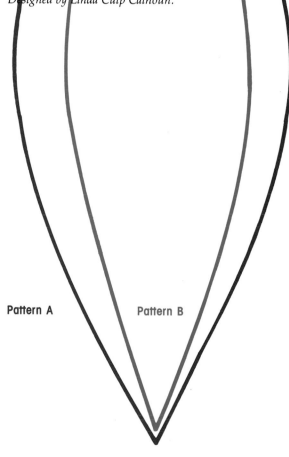

Pattern A   Pattern B

holiday Heritage

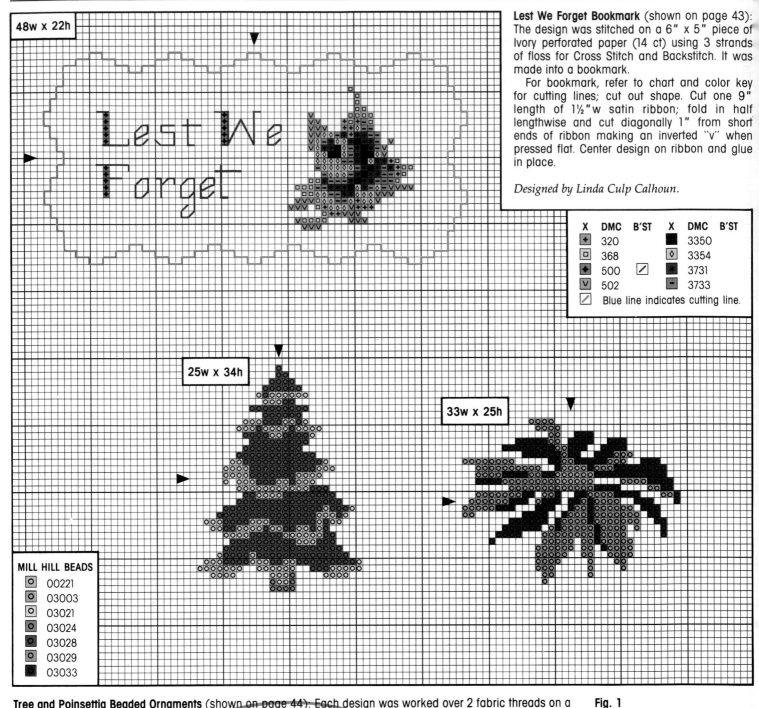

48w x 22h

Lest We Forget Bookmark (shown on page 43): The design was stitched on a 6" x 5" piece of Ivory perforated paper (14 ct) using 3 strands of floss for Cross Stitch and Backstitch. It was made into a bookmark.

For bookmark, refer to chart and color key for cutting lines; cut out shape. Cut one 9" length of 1½"w satin ribbon; fold in half lengthwise and cut diagonally 1" from short ends of ribbon making an inverted "v" when pressed flat. Center design on ribbon and glue in place.

Designed by Linda Culp Calhoun.

X	DMC	B'ST	X	DMC	B'ST
+	320		■	3350	
□	368		◇	3354	
✦	500	/	✳	3731	
V	502		-	3733	
/	Blue line indicates cutting line.				

25w x 34h

33w x 25h

MILL HILL BEADS
- 00221
- 03003
- 03021
- 03024
- 03028
- 03029
- 03033

Tree and Poinsettia Beaded Ornaments (shown on page 44): Each design was worked over 2 fabric threads on a 7" square of Raw Belfast Linen (32 ct). They were made into stuffed ornaments.

For attaching beads to fabric, refer to chart for bead placement and sew bead in place using sewing thread and a fine needle that will pass through bead. Bring needle up through fabric, run needle through bead then down through fabric making a Half Cross Stitch as shown in **Fig. 1**. Secure thread on back or move to next bead.

For each ornament, fold sheet of tracing paper in half. Place fold of paper on dashed line of pattern and trace pattern onto tracing paper; cut out pattern. Unfold pattern and press flat. Center pattern on right side of beaded design and draw around pattern on fabric with fabric marking pencil; cut out shape. Cut same size piece of Belfast Linen for backing; set aside.

Cut one 14" length of ¼" dia. cording; if needed, trim seam allowance to ¼". Beginning and ending at bottom of design and starting ½" from end of cording, baste cording to beaded design matching right sides and raw edges. Overlap ends of cording and tack in place; trim excess cording. Use zipper foot and ¼" seam allowance to sew cording to beaded design. Matching right sides and leaving an opening for turning and stuffing, use a zipper foot and a ¼" seam allowance to sew beaded design and backing fabric together. Clip curves and turn ornament right side out, stuff ornament with polyester fiberfill and whipstitch opening closed.

Designed by Linda Culp Calhoun.

Fig. 1

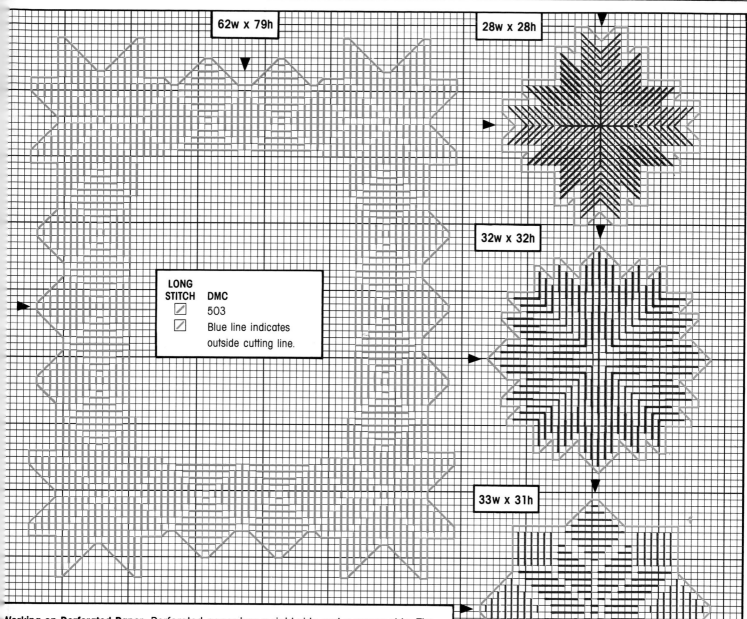

62w x 79h

28w x 28h

32w x 32h

33w x 31h

LONG
STITCH **DMC**

☑ 503

☑ Blue line indicates outside cutting line.

Working on Perforated Paper: Perforated paper has a right side and a wrong side. The right side is smoother and stitching should be done on this side. To find the center, do not fold paper; use a ruler and mark lightly with a pencil or count holes. Perforated paper will tear if handled roughly; therefore, hold paper flat while stitching and do not use a hoop. Begin and end stitching by running floss under several stitches on back; never tie knots. Use the stab method when stitching and keep stitching tension consistent. Thread pulled too tightly may tear the paper. Carry floss across back as little as possible.

Large Perforated Paper Frames (shown on pages 44-45) **and Small Perforated Paper Frames** (shown on page 42): Each design was stitched using 3 strands of floss for Cross Stitch and Long Stitch and 2 strands for Backstitch. Large frames were each stitched on a 9" x 12" piece of Ivory perforated paper (14 ct), and small frames were each stitched on a 5" x 7" piece of Brown perforated paper (14 ct). They were made into photo frames.

To finish each photo frame, refer to chart and color key for outside cutting line. Measure desired photo to be inserted in each frame to determine inside cutting line.

For each photo frame backing, cut one piece of perforated paper ¼" larger on all sides than desired photo measurement. Center backing on wrong side of photo frame and glue side and bottom edges in place.

Designed by Kathy Elrod.

Perforated Paper Ornaments (shown on page 45): Each design was stitched on a 4" square of Brown perforated paper (14 ct) using 3 strands of floss for Long Stitch. They were made into ornaments.

For each ornament, refer to photo to alternate colors of floss in designs as desired (we used DMC 304 - lt red, DMC 501 - dk green, DMC 503 - lt green, and DMC 814 - dk red). To finish ornament, refer to chart for cutting lines indicated by blue lines on chart.

For each hanger, cut a 6" length of desired color ribbon, knot ends together and glue knot to back of ornament.

Designed by Arlene K. Jacobson.

Perforated Paper Frames
Instructions on page 83.

93w x 138h

54w x 66h

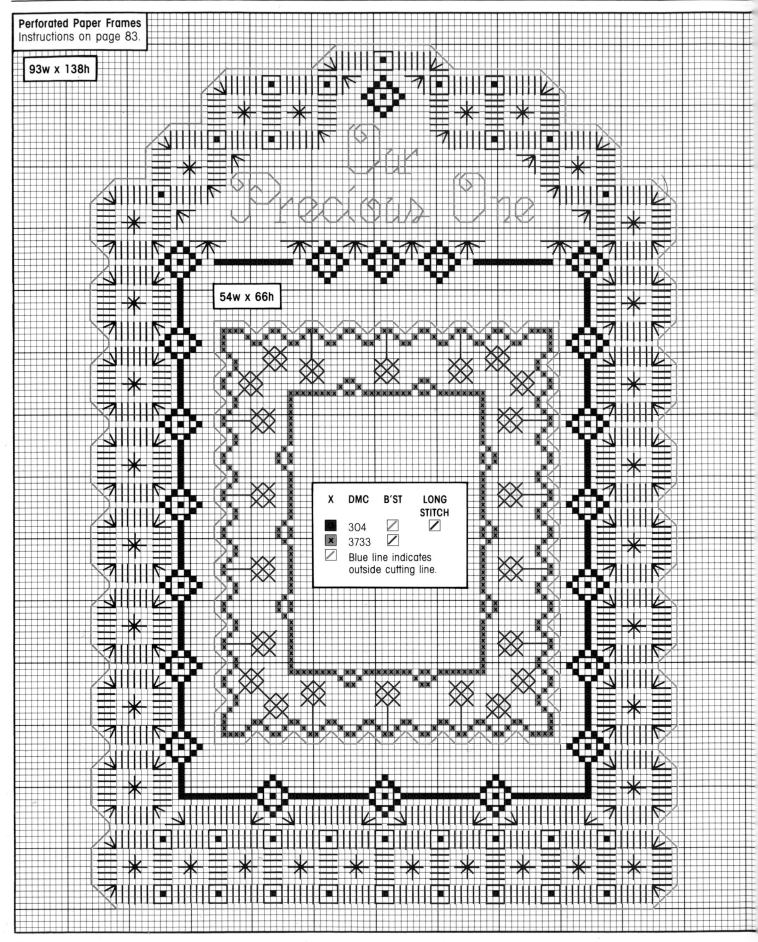

X	DMC	B'ST	LONG STITCH
■	304	╱	╱
✕	3733	╱	
╱	Blue line indicates outside cutting line.		

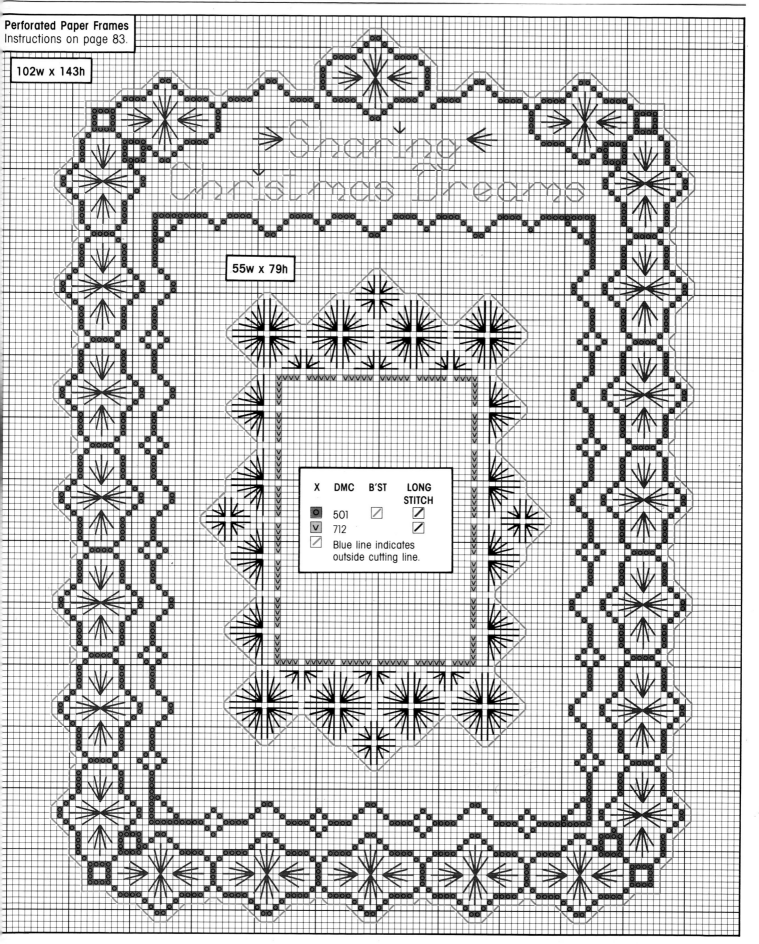

Perforated Paper Frames
Instructions on page 83.

102w x 143h

55w x 79h

X	DMC	B'ST	LONG STITCH
●	501	/	/
V	712		/
/	Blue line indicates outside cutting line.		

fanciful flower Girls

Flower Girl Ornaments (shown on page 22): Each design was stitched over 2 fabric threads on a 6" square of Cream Belfast Linen (32 ct). Two strands of floss were used for Cross Stitch and 1 strand for Backstitch. They were inserted in artificial flowers.

Trace pattern onto tracing paper; cut out pattern. For each Flower Girl, center pattern on right side of stitched piece and draw around pattern; cut out. Thread needle with a 20" length of six-strand embroidery floss and baste ½" from raw edge of stitched piece. Pull ends of floss to gather stitched piece; firmly stuff with polyester fiberfill. Pull floss ends tight and knot to secure. Apply a generous amount of liquid fray preventative to raw edges of stitched piece (up to basting line); allow to dry. Trim raw edges ⅛" from basting line; clip excess floss ends.

If necessary, remove center of artificial flower. Refer to photo and hot glue stitched piece to inside center of flower. Trim stem of flower to desired length.

Needlework adaptation by Carol Emmer.

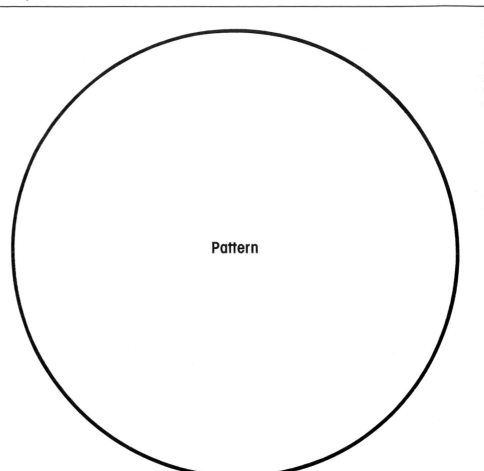

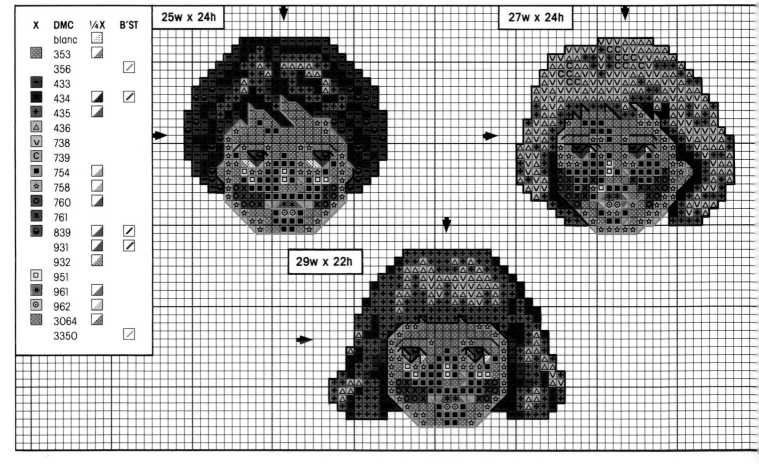

holy night nativity

Nativity Figures (shown on pages 34-35): Each design was stitched on Dirty Aida (14 ct). Three strands of floss were used for Cross Stitch and 1 strand for all other stitches. To attach beads, refer to chart for bead placement and sew bead in place using nylon line and a fine needle that will pass through the bead. The designs were made into stuffed figures.

For each stuffed figure, cut a piece of Aida same size as stitched piece for backing. Matching right sides and raw edges and leaving bottom edge open, sew stitched piece and backing together ⅛" from design as shown in **Fig. 1**. Leaving a ¼" seam allowance, cut out figure. Clip seam allowances at curves; turn figure right side out and carefully push curves outward. Trim bottom edge of figure ½" from bottom of design. Press raw edges ¼" to wrong side; stuff figure with polyester fiberfill up to 1½" from opening.

Fig. 1

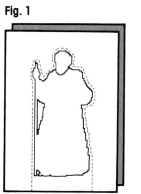

For base, set figure on tracing paper and draw around base of figure. Add a ½" seam allowance to pattern; cut out. Place pattern on a piece of Aida. Use fabric marking pencil to draw around pattern; cut out along drawn line. Baste around base piece ½" from raw edge; press raw edges to wrong side along basting line.

To weight bottom of figure, fill a plastic sandwich bag with a small amount of aquarium gravel. Place bag of gravel into opening of figure.

Pin wrong side of base piece over opening. Whipstitch in place, adding polyester fiberfill as necessary to fill bottom of figure. Remove basting threads.

Designed by Carol Emmer.

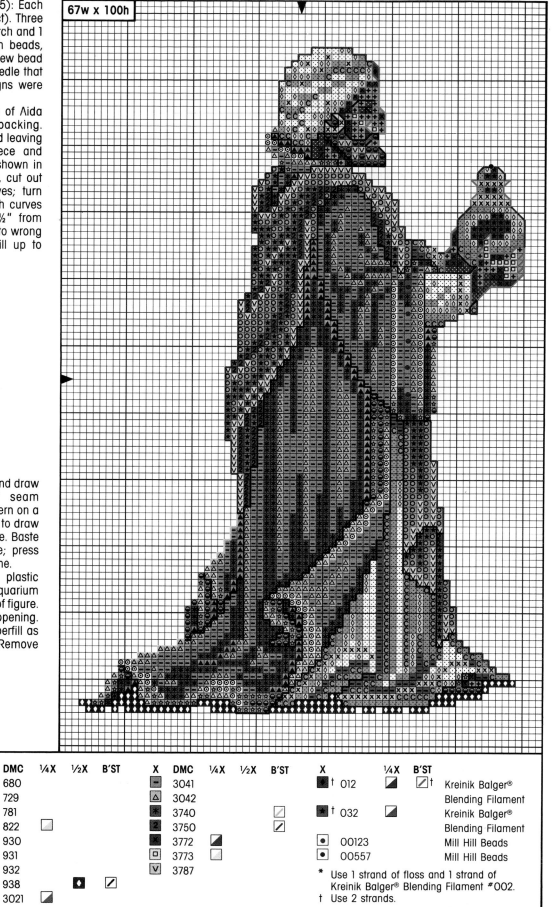

67w x 100h

X	DMC	¼X	½X	B'ST		X	DMC	¼X	½X	B'ST		X	DMC	¼X	½X	B'ST		X		¼X	B'ST	
	blanc			◪		☆	680					━	3041					◆ †	012	◪	◪†	Kreinik Balger®
✦	407	◪				△	729					△	3042									Blending Filament
▲	535			◪		◉	781					✳	3740		◪			★ †	032	◪	◪	Kreinik Balger®
▨	632	◪		◪		◇	822			☐		2	3750		◪							Blending Filament
━	640					★	930					✕	3772	◪				●	00123			Mill Hill Beads
C	642	◪				◯	931					☐	3773	◪				●	00557			Mill Hill Beads
	644	◪				V	932					V	3787									
◉	676						938		◪	◪								* Use 1 strand of floss and 1 strand of Kreinik Balger® Blending Filament #002.				
✕ *	676	◪		◪ *		◉	3021	◪										† Use 2 strands.				

holy night nativity

Nativity Figures
Instructions on page 87.

60w x 84h

47w x 101h

X	DMC	¼X	½X	B'ST		X	DMC	¼X	½X	B'ST		X	DMC	¼X	½X	B'ST		X	DMC	¼X	½X	B'ST
	blanc			╱			640			╱		◇	760					✚	930	╱		
■	221	◣		╱		C	642	╱				✱	780			╱		◉	931	╱		
★	319	◣				✱	644	╱					781	◢				V	932			
2	320	◣				V	676					R	782					■	938		⊠	╱
V	353	╱				◇*	676					◆	783						948	╱		
	356		╱			4	677					◇*	783	◣				△	3045	╱		
◆	367					★	680	◣				◇	801			╱†		★	3064	╱		
▲	368					◒*	725			╱*		-	822		╱			◯	3328			
	420	◢				2	729	╱				■	869			╱†		✕	3712	◣		
◉	422	╱				H	754	╱					890			╱		▬	3721	◣		
	632					✚	758	◣				◆	902	╱		╱						

49w x 102h

48w x 30h

70w x 79h

X	DMC	¼X	½X	B'ST
	3750			
	031	Kreinik Balger® Blending Filament		
●	03003	Mill Hill beads		
●	00557	Mill Hill beads		

* Use 1 strand of floss and
1 strand of Kreinik Balger®
Blending Filament #002.

† Use 801 for Joseph. Use
869 for Baby Jesus and
Mary.

holy night nativity

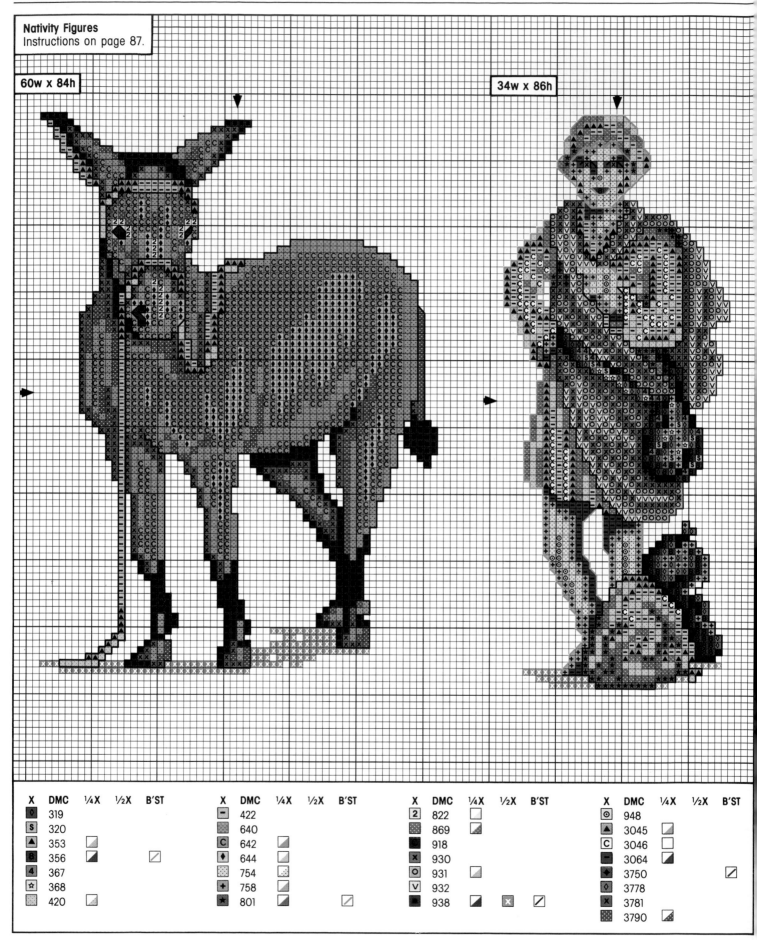

Nativity Figures
Instructions on page 87.

60w x 84h

34w x 86h

X	DMC	¼X	½X	B'ST		X	DMC	¼X	½X	B'ST		X	DMC	¼X	½X	B'ST		X	DMC	¼X	½X	B'ST
◊	319					−	422					2	822					◉	948			
S	320						640						869					▲	3045			
▲	353					C	642						918					C	3046			
8	356					◆	644					✕	930					−	3064			
4	367						754					O	931					◆	3750			
☆	368					+	758					V	932					◊	3778			
	420					★	801					■	938					✕	3781			
																		3790			

90

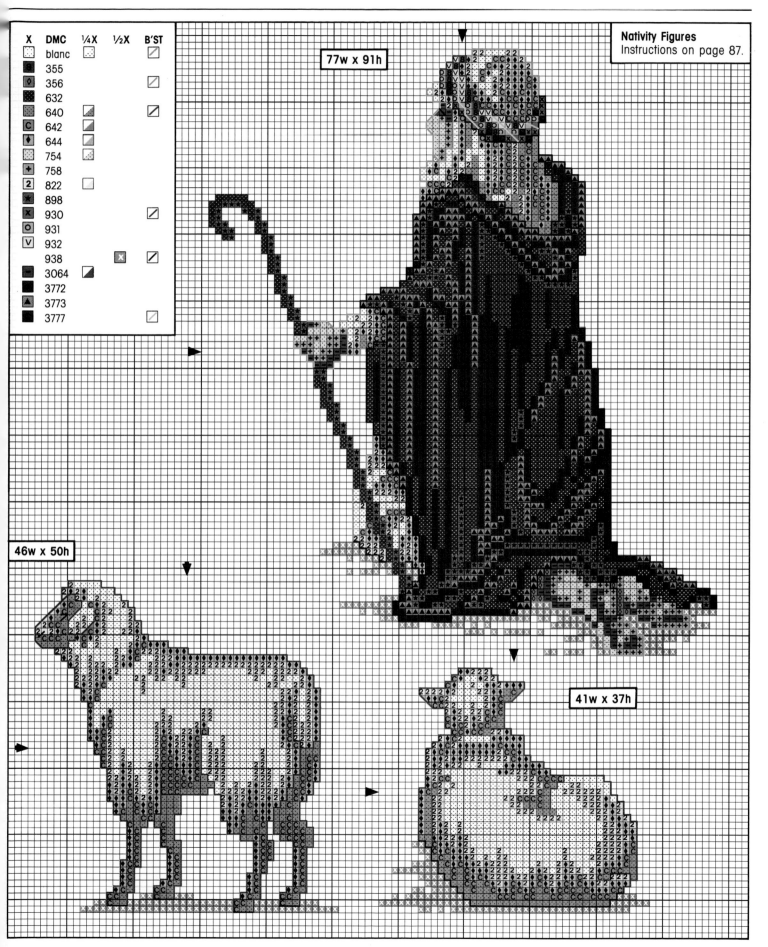

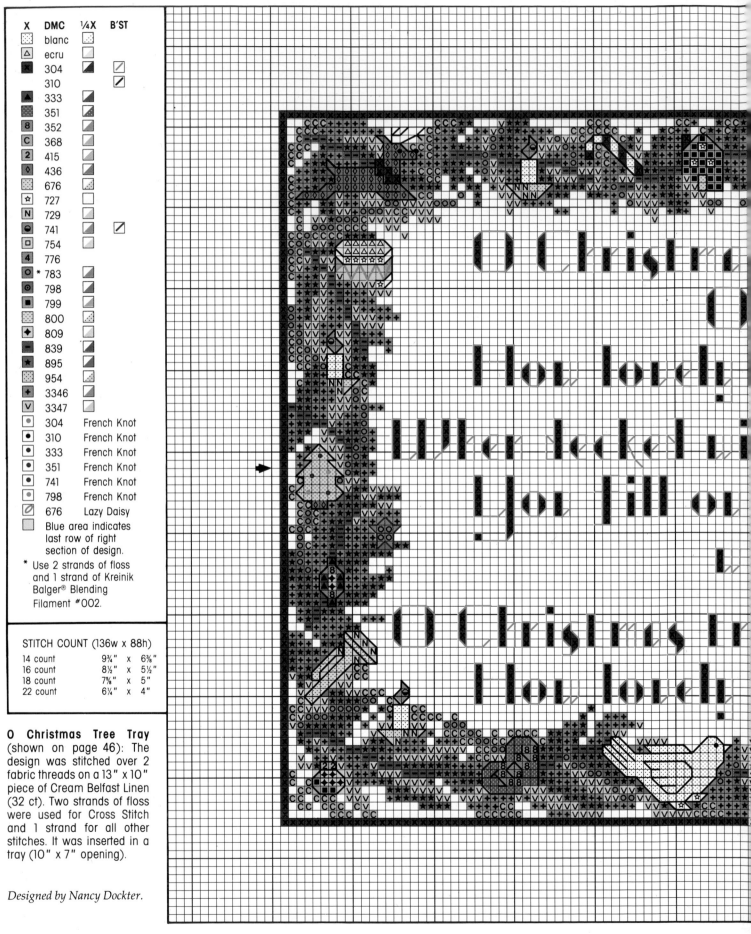

X	DMC	¼X	B'ST
	blanc		
△	ecru		
✖	304		⟋
	310		⟋
▲	333		
	351		
8	352		
C	368		
2	415		
◇	436		
	676		
☆	727		
N	729		
⊙	741		⟋
▢	754		
4	776		
O	* 783		
◉	798		
■	799		
	800		
◆	809		
▬	839		
★	895		
	954		
+	3346		
V	3347		
•	304	French Knot
•	310	French Knot
•	333	French Knot
•	351	French Knot
•	741	French Knot
•	798	French Knot
⬿	676	Lazy Daisy
		Blue area indicates last row of right section of design.

* Use 2 strands of floss and 1 strand of Kreinik Balger® Blending Filament #002.

STITCH COUNT (136w x 88h)

14 count	9¾"	x	6¾"
16 count	8½"	x	5½"
18 count	7⅝"	x	5"
22 count	6¼"	x	4"

O Christmas Tree Tray (shown on page 46): The design was stitched over 2 fabric threads on a 13" x 10" piece of Cream Belfast Linen (32 ct). Two strands of floss were used for Cross Stitch and 1 strand for all other stitches. It was inserted in a tray (10" x 7" opening).

Designed by Nancy Dockter.

the Gracious Evergreen

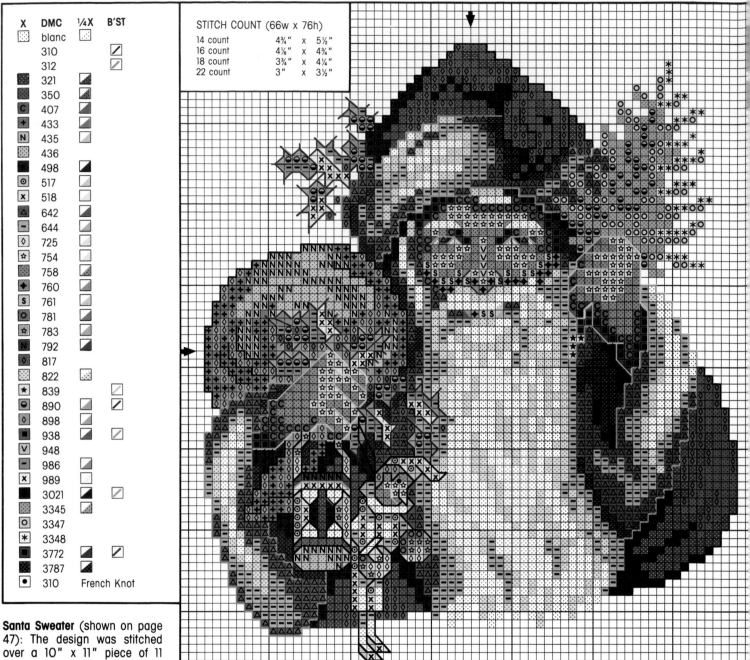

X	DMC	¼X	B'ST
	blanc		
	310		╱
	312		╱
	321	◥	
	350	◥	
C	407	◥	
+	433	◥	
N	435	◥	
	436		
☉	498	◥	
	517	◥	
x	518		
△	642	◥	
—	644		
◇	725	◥	
☆	754		
	758	◥	
◆	760	◥	
S	761	◥	
○	781	◥	
☆	783	◥	
N	792	◥	
◊	817		
	822	◹	
★	839		╱
◉	890	◥	╱
◇	898	◥	
■	938	◥	╱
V	948		
—	986		
x	989		
■	3021	◥	╱
	3345	◥	
○	3347		
*	3348		
■	3772	◥	╱
	3787	◥	
●	310	French Knot	

STITCH COUNT (66w x 76h)			
14 count	4¾"	x	5½"
16 count	4⅛"	x	4¾"
18 count	3¾"	x	4¼"
22 count	3"	x	3½"

Santa Sweater (shown on page 47): The design was stitched over a 10" x 11" piece of 11 mesh waste canvas on a purchased sweater with top of design approx. 1½" below bottom of neckband. Six strands of floss were used for Cross Stitch and 2 strands for all other stitches.

For snowflakes, remove waste canvas and randomly attach Mill Hill Beads #03021 to sweater using 1 strand of ecru embroidery floss.

Needlework adaptation by Nancy Dockter.

Working on Waste Canvas: Waste canvas is a special canvas that provides an evenweave grid for placing stitches on fabric. After the design is worked over the canvas, the canvas threads are removed leaving the design on the fabric. The canvas is available in several mesh sizes.

Cover edges of canvas with masking tape. Cut a piece of lightweight, non-fusible interfacing the same size as canvas to provide a firm stitching base.

Find desired stitching area on sweater and mark center of area with a pin. Match center of canvas to pin. Use the blue threads in canvas to place canvas straight on sweater; pin canvas to sweater. P▮ interfacing to wrong side of sweater. Baste all three thicknesse▮ together as shown in **Fig. 1**.

Place sweater in a screw type hoop. We recommend a hoop that ▮ large enough to encircle entire design. Using a sharp needle, wor▮ design, stitching from large holes to large holes.

Trim canvas to within ¾" of design. Dampen canvas until ▮ becomes limp. Pull out canvas threads one at a time using tweeze▮ (**Fig. 2**). Trim interfacing close to design.

Fig. 1   **Fig. 2**

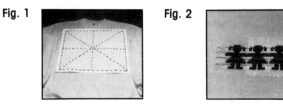

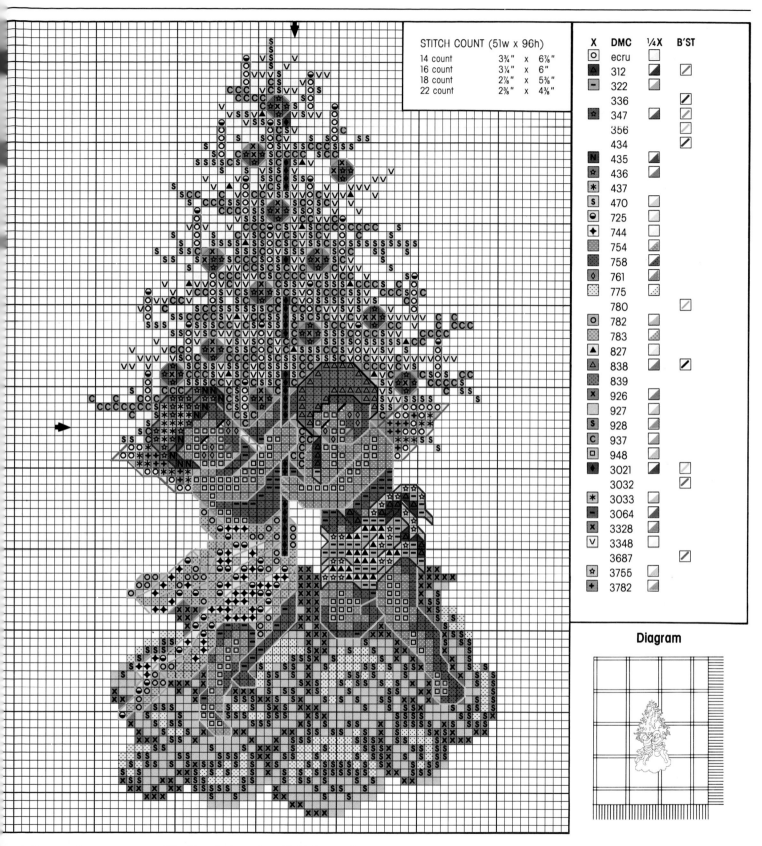

X	DMC	¼X	B'ST
⊙	ecru		
▲	312	◪	☑
-	322	◪	
	336		☑
☆	347	◪	☑
	356		☑
	434		☑
N	435	◪	
☆	436	◪	
*	437		
S	470	◻	
◒	725		
◆	744		
	754	◨	
	758	◪	
◇	761	◪	
▦	775	◪	
	780		☑
○	782	◪	
▦	783	◪	
▲	827	◪	
△	838	◪	☑
	839	◪	
X	926	◪	
	927	◪	
S	928	◪	
C	937	◪	
◻	948	◪	
◆	3021	◪	☑
	3032		☑
*	3033	◪	
-	3064	◪	
X	3328	◪	
V	3348	◻	
	3687		☑
☆	3755	◪	
◆	3782	◪	

STITCH COUNT (51w x 96h)

14 count	3¾" x 6⅞"
16 count	3¼" x 6"
18 count	2⅞" x 5⅜"
22 count	2⅜" x 4⅜"

Diagram

Angel Afghan (shown on page 47): The design was stitched over 2 fabric threads on a 45"x 58" piece of Ivory Anne Cloth (18 ct). It was made into an afghan.

For afghan, cut off selvages of fabric; measure 5½" from raw edge of fabric and pull out 1 fabric thread. Fringe fabric up to missing fabric thread. Repeat for each side. Tie an overhand knot at each corner with 4 horizontal and 4 vertical fabric threads. Working from corners, use 8 fabric threads for each knot until all threads are knotted.

Refer to Diagram for placement of design on fabric; use 6 strands of floss for Cross Stitch and 2 strands for Backstitch.

Needlework adaptation by Jane Chandler.

95

GENERAL INSTRUCTIONS

WORKING WITH CHARTS

How to Read Charts: Each of the designs is shown in chart form. Each colored square on the chart represents one Cross Stitch or one Half Cross Stitch. Each colored triangle on the chart represents one Quarter Stitch. Black or colored dots represent French Knots. Colored ovals represent Lazy Daisy Stitches. The black or colored straight lines on the chart indicate Backstitch. When a French Knot, Lazy Daisy Stitch, or Backstitch covers a square, the symbol is omitted.

Each chart is accompanied by a color key. This key indicates the color of floss to use for each stitch on the chart. The headings on the color key are for Cross Stitch (**X**), DMC color number (**DMC**), One-Quarter Stitch (**¼X**), Half Cross Stitch (**½X**), and Backstitch (**B'ST**). Color key columns should be read vertically and horizontally to determine type of stitch and floss color.

STITCH DIAGRAMS

Counted Cross Stitch (X): Work one Cross Stitch to correspond to each colored square on the chart. For horizontal rows, work stitches in two journeys (**Fig. 1**). For vertical rows, complete each stitch as shown (**Fig. 2**). When working over two fabric threads, work Cross Stitch as shown in **Fig. 3**. When the chart shows a Backstitch crossing a colored square (**Fig. 4**), a Cross Stitch should be worked first; then the Backstitch (**Fig. 9** or **10**) should be worked on top of the Cross Stitch.

Fig. 1

Fig. 2

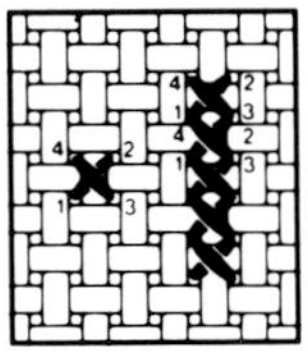

Fig. 3

Fig. 4

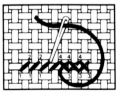

Quarter Stitch (¼X): Quarter Stitches are denoted by triangular shapes of color on the chart and on the color key. Come up at 1 (**Fig. 5**); then split fabric thread to go down at 2. **Fig. 6** shows the technique for Quarter Stitch when working over two fabric threads.

Fig. 5

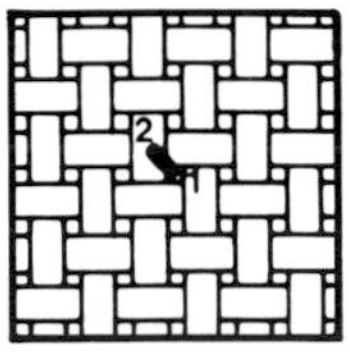

Fig. 6

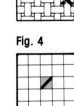

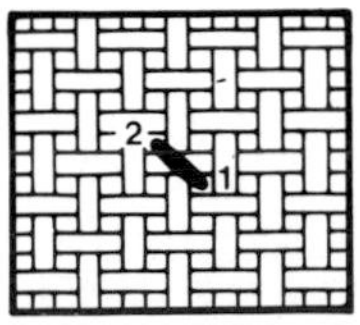

Half Cross Stitch (½X): This stitch is one journey of the Cross Stitch and is worked from lower left to upper right as shown in **Fig. 7**. When working over two fabric threads, work Half Cross Stitch as shown in **Fig. 8**.

Fig. 7

Fig. 8

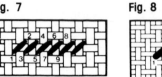

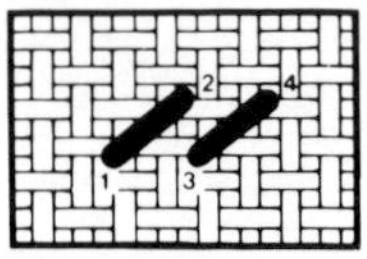

Backstitch (B'ST): For outline detail, Backstitch (shown on chart and on color key by black or colored straight lines) should be worked after the design has been completed (**Fig. 9**). When working over two fabric threads, work Backstitch as shown in **Fig. 10**.

Fig. 9

Fig. 10

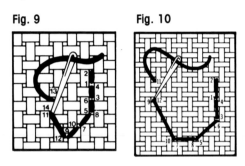

French Knot: Bring needle up at 1. Wrap floss once around needle and insert needle at 2, holding end of floss with non-stitching fingers (**Fig. 11**). Tighten knot; then pull needle through fabric, holding floss until it must be released. For larger knot, use more strands; wrap only once.

Fig. 11

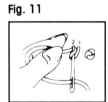

Lazy Daisy Stitch: Bring needle up at 1 and make a loop. Go down at 1 and come up at 2, keeping floss below point of needle (**Fig. 12**). Pull needle through and go down at 2 to anchor loop, completing stitch. (**Note:** To support stitches, it may be helpful to go down in edge of next fabric thread when anchoring loop.)

Fig. 12

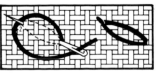

Long Stitch: The Long Stitch can be worked vertically, diagonally, or horizontally (**Fig. 13**). The number of holes each stitch is worked over may vary according to the chart.

Fig. 13

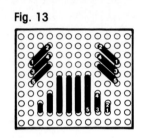

STITCHING TIP

Working Over Two Fabric Threads: Use the sewing method instead of the stab method when working over two fabric threads. To use the sewing method, keep your stitching hand on the right side of the fabric (instead of stabbing the fabric with the needle and taking your stitching hand to the back of the fabric to pick up the needle). With the sewing method, you take the needle down and up with one stroke instead of two. To add support to stitches, it is important that the first Cross Stitch is placed on the fabric with stitch 1-2 beginning and ending where a vertical fabric thread crosses over a horizontal fabric thread (**Fig. 14**). When the first stitch is in the correct position, the entire design will be placed properly, with vertical fabric threads supporting each stitch.

Fig. 14

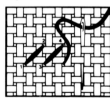

Instructions tested and photo items made by Janet Akins, Debbie Barrett, Debbie Bashaw, Vicki Bishop, Deborah Burns, Mary Carlton, Carrie Clifford, Natalie DeAngelo, Anita Drennan, Nannette Easterling, Tamara Easterling, Kathy Elrod, Marilyn Fendley, Joyce Graves, Cara Lea Gregory, Chrys Harvey, Muriel Hicks, Barbara Hodges, Ginny Hogue, Joyce Holland, Pat Johnson, Pat Jones, Kathy Kampbell, Vanessa Kiihnl, Velda Lawrence, Melanie Long, Margaret Mosely, Debbie Newkirk, Martha Nolan, Tish O'Neil, Mary Phinney, Sandy Pigue, Susan Sego, Lavonne L. Sims, Lee Ann Smith, Opal Steen, Kay Szafranski, Amy Taylor, Karen Tyler, Patricia Vines, Jane Walker, Sharon Walker, Karey Weeks, Marie P. Williford, and Janie Wright.